ADVANCED PRAISE FOR

*"This book is a deeply necessary offering. Fawn illuminates a healing path rooted in wisdom and a joyous reclaiming of rest as resistance. Her words call out toxic systems that demand our exhaustion and invite us to disrupt those cycles with spiritual alignment. Fawn's writing is for those who are ready to answer the call of our dear ancestors through rituals and self-love.*

~Julius Boatwright, Licensed Clinical Social Worker
Founder and Managing Director, Steel Smiling

*Fawn Walker-Montgomery's story cuts to the heart of the matter of too many Black women whose voices are ignored and discounted by the Medical System. The glaring message in this book is one of advocacy and agency of one's body, which is the highest form of self-care.*

~Dr. Y, Fálámi Devoe
Self-Care Ritualist/ Healing Justice Practitioner

*Fawn takes you through deep human life experiences and struggles within the perilous world of politics, medical misdiagnosis, systemic challenges, mental health, and growth. This is a heartfelt, vulnerable, and authentic understanding towards rediscovering oneself and the importance of knowing the impact of the past upon the present and future. We can't continue walking through life "With Our Eyes Closed."*

~Dr. Valerie J. Harper, M. Ed, Former Law School Registrar
for Duquesne University and Diversity Specialist

*Empathy and compassion are important because people are fighting battles we know nothing about. In Healing in the Fight, Fawn pulls back the curtain to show us the warrior without her armor and the hidden battle that fuels the visible one.*

~Penda L. James, M. Ed.
Scribe Coach, InSCRIBEd Inspiration

*Prepare to sit courtside as Fawn explains how she's finding peace with her forever thorn, endometriosis. You'll learn about her growth in health, relationships, and even spirituality. Although we've seen Fawn "The Superhero" advocate and fight for so many, this book will help you to understand Fawn "The Human." You'll appreciate her even more for every sacrifice, and her evolution to champion for her "Highest Self."*

~Natalie Reid Master's Level Education Specialist, Editor, and Former Teacher

*It feels like a love letter to survivors living with endometriosis and chronic pain (physical, emotional, and spiritual). I've lived with endometriosis for 25 years, and wish I had access to her book much earlier in my journey. If you suffer from endometriosis, or someone in your life is impacted by chronic pain or illness, this book will be a beautiful gift for curating a multidisciplinary, spiritual care practice that expands beyond the cookie cutter symptom-fix approach, to one steeped in love, tailored to meet your needs.*

~Ebony Ross, Principal, Ebony Ross Consulting and Endo Warrior/Survivor

# Healing In The FIGHT

# Healing In The FIGHT

### A Black Woman's Journey With Endometriosis and Radical Self-Care

## Fawn Walker-Montgomery

# DEDICATION

To the **Most High, elders, my family, close friends, and community.**

To my **Ancestors** who weren't allowed to be soft; those who dared to reimagine a different life and resist. All who have inspired me along my healing journey.

My **Mother, Myrna Lloyd-Gould**, taught me how to advocate, she has always constantly supported me. She was the first person to teach me about endometriosis.

To everyone battling the horrible disease of endometriosis and those who became ancestors due to endometriosis: **Aubrion Rogers, Mary Njambi Koikai, and all the names both known and unknown.**

**Special dedication to Black women who've had to be strong.** Embrace the awkward, weird, soft, and calm parts of yourself. There isn't a reward for being the most effective, productive, or toughest. I hope this book inspires you to rest, resist, and put yourself first! ASE.

## ACKNOWLEDGEMENTS

**To my daughter**, **Grace,** who inspires me to fight, live, and strive to be a better person. **My husband, George**, whose support reminds me to dream, rest, and be soft. **My best friend, Natalie**, thanks for being a rock and a constant source of support. **My healing process** has taught me about myself and my **ancestral lineage.**

I now truly understand what it means to say, **"I'm the daughter of Myrna Lloyd Gould, granddaughter of Grace Herriott Lloyd, and great-granddaughter of Helen Savage Herriott-Briscoe."** I'll highlight how I drew from their examples of strength and vulnerability throughout this book.

**This love letter to myself** is a reminder not to forget my power to heal myself and my community. It emphasizes it's okay to rest and be soft, and tells folks who I am: a proud Black woman, mother, wife, community organizer, healer, and activist.

# CONTENTS

Foreword......................................................... xiii

Introduction ................................................. xv

Fawny Boo Boo ...............................................1

A Child Navigating Gyno Experiences..................... 13

Stoic ............................................................ 21

Endo Cycle Continues ................................. 25

Becoming Hood Famous ............................... 35

Politics And Community Work................................. 45

Unlearning White Supremacy ...................... 55

The Body Keeps Score: I'm More Than Labor........ 65

Medical Advocacy And Stage 4 Endometriosis........ 75

Embracing The Journey To My Higher Self............. 87

Radical Self-Care.......................................... 99

Endo: The Gift That Keeps On Giving ................. 113

Not Fighting My Pivot.................................................. 121

Healing At My Kitchen Table: Nurturing My

Community..................................................................... 127

Advocacy And Resources........................................... 133

New Tools And Tips ................................................... 135

Conclusion .................................................................... 141

Appendix............................................................................. 143

References.................................................................... 149

Glossary........................................................................ 153

About The Author............................................................ 159

# FOREWORD

Fawn Walker-Montgomery is a force. I've known her for around two years through community work; I'm so happy and proud of her for being vulnerable and using her pain to inspire others. Fawn is a prolific activist, compassionate community organizer, devoted mother, loving wife, and now, a courageous author. *Healing in the Fight* is Fawn's unflinching and deeply vulnerable offering to the world. It is a testimony, a teaching, and a triumph.

Fawn invites us into the most intimate corners of her life, her battle with endometriosis, her unrelenting dedication to activism, and her complex journey through Black womanhood in America. With raw honesty and bold transparency, she explores what it means to live in a body that's been her battleground and source of power.

Fawn is loud when the world tells Black women to be quiet. She is bold in the face of pressure to shrink. She is everything "they" tell us not to be and that's what

xiv

makes her voice so necessary, so electric, and so healing. Her story is not only her own, but also a mirror, a map, and a movement.

There is so much that remains misunderstood, dismissed, or hidden when it comes to endometriosis and the lived experience of Black women navigating chronic pain, systemic injustice, and the toll of constant resistance. Fawn declares, "No more." She rises, and in doing so, makes room for us to rise with her.

This book is a call to radical self-care, rootedness, and truth-telling. Fawn reminds us that healing isn't passive. It's a fight, and one we're worthy of winning. Her journey is riveting and heart-quenching, and her voice rings like freedom on every page.

Prepare to be challenged. Prepare to be seen. And most of all, prepare to heal.

~Michelle Cooley, LCSW,

Co-owner, Living in Confidence Counseling Services

# INTRODUCTION

My passion for **Black liberation** stems from supporting my community and advocating for social justice as well as racial equality. I mention Black liberation a lot throughout the book, so I want to take the time to explain what it means to me:

*A strong and genuine commitment to the safety and liberation of all Black people, promoting Black aligned leadership and Black-centered community transformations.*

A significant part of my work around this is centered around my hometown of McKeesport, Pennsylvania, in the Greater Pittsburgh area of Allegheny County.

Growing up in a small town, my experiences with racial organizing have deeply shaped my life's path. This, in turn, led me to embark on a healing journey rooted in radical self-care and ancestral healing. Throughout the book I use the words "radical" and "self-care" together and separately.

For me, "radical" means to push for change even when it's not popular and push against the status quo. While self-care involves taking care of your physical, emotional, and spiritual health. However, doing self-care alone can at times be surface level and is often pushed as spa trips. Adding the word "radical" pushes for it to be a different and more extreme form of care. Throughout the book I go into detail about how this looks for me.

That's what makes this memoir a living biography or personal chronicle of sorts. While reading it you may laugh, cry, and learn how to advocate for yourself, support loved ones dealing with endometriosis, and gain education on the condition. This includes highlighting the use of hoodoo, ancestral healing, and CBD as treatment options, while placing a spotlight on the challenges that Black women with endometriosis face. I explore my healing journey with endometriosis and how has shaped, and affected my fight for Black liberation.*

Before we dive in, just a heads-up: Endometriosis is an unforgiving and, at times, raw disease. It is a painful condition (mostly during periods), and it can cause tissue, similar to the inner lining of the uterus, to grow outside the uterus. Additionally, I am a raw and honest person. So, if you're not a fan of profanity, this may not be the book for you, lol.

I also do my work at the intersection of revolutionary socialism, racial justice, environmental justice, and Black queer feminism. You will see that throughout the book. Vulnerability is a new experience for me, but it has been healing and has become one of my superpowers. So, without further ado, here we go with my endo story.

**READY, START, GO!**

# *DISCLAIMER

The methods presented in this book are intended as suggestions and should not be considered medical advice. Always consult a qualified healthcare professional before making any health-related decisions.

xx

*Endometriosis is an unforgiving and,*

*at times, raw disease.*

~Fawn Walker-Montgomery

# FAWNY BOO BOO

To start things off, we need to go back to the beginning where my fight for **Black liberation** began; we also need to go back to the time I first experienced the ancestors, racialization, and the start of my battle with endometriosis.

In my early childhood, my mother was raising me and my brother alone. This was after  she ended an abusive relationship with my biological Father. They had been together since high school and the relationship became toxic. I don't remember the abuse, but my brother does. He witnessed it as well. The only thing I remember is seeing some scars on my Mother. She gained the courage to leave him and connected my brother with a program to talk about what he saw growing up.

In my later years my Father and I would reconnect and repair our relationship. However, my Mother raised us as a single parent until she met my stepfather when I was around 5. My Mother worked various jobs at fast food restaurants, so we often stayed with my grandparents.

I affectionally called them "Granny" and "Pap Pap." They were instrumental in my childhood and rocks for our entire family. My maternal grandfather, Robert "Grayeagle" Lloyd was a consistent father figure. He's the one who gave me the nickname "Fawny Boo Boo."

## Robert "Pap Pap" Lloyd

My Pap Pap's name is Robert Lloyd. His friends, family, and some of his colleagues called him "Grayeagle" because he had been a great baseball player in his younger years. Pap Pap was known to have a strong pitching arm.

I have fond memories of Pap Pap making silly faces and dancing, which made me laugh. He and my granny, Grace Herriott Loyd, were married for over 50 years. They loved to dance together, and we often made dances for them during the holidays. On Sundays, we sometimes went to our family church, St. Paul African American Methodist Episcopal (AME) because they were active members there.

## Racism, Pap Pap and Me

I remember Pap Pap being strong, focused, and a good provider, having served McKeesport as a longtime public works employee. We never talked about his experiences with racism in athletics, or in McKeesport, but I know that he endured various instances of it. He worked for the City of McKeesport public works department for years. I remember him telling his friends about white people at work giving him a hard time. Specifically, writing him up for everything and not paying an adequate wage. Additionally, Pap Pap's extraordinary baseball talents were not recognized beyond McKeesport because of racism. Unfortunately, this is a familiar story for many ancestors who played baseball.

My first memory of dealing with racism was around nine years old, when we started learning about slavery in school. I remember feeling upset, and immediately, my stomach started to hurt. I would later learn that this was the beginning of racism showing up in my body. After school, I went home and talked to my stepdad; he worked the night shift, and my mom was at work. When I told him how I felt about the slavery discussion, he validated my feelings and explained the history of racism. He introduced me to the Black Panthers, Malcolm X, and Public Enemy. I watched Public Enemy on TV and remember thinking, "It is powerful to see Black people being unapologetically proud." My stepdad instilled in me the importance of fighting for my people.

Not long after, our family began to experience racism from our neighbors, being called the n-word, among other things. My mother and other relatives handled it swiftly, but I was upset. I was so young, yet I remember feeling so much anger. I continued to read about Black liberation, not knowing how much I would need that knowledge just a year later.

In middle school, we were reading "Huckleberry Finn," and they kept saying the N-word in the book. Me and the other Black students in the class were upset. I told my parents, "I am mad about this book!"

They challenged me, "Do something about it."

With their guidance, I went to the principal and advocated for the book to be removed from the curriculum. It worked, and that was my first experience seeing how powerful it was to speak truth to power.

## Pap Pap Becomes An Ancestor

When I was ten, Pap Pap had a heart attack while he was driving to work. As we were preparing to go to school, my mother got a phone call and started screaming a few seconds after she answered. As she ran out of the house, she told my brother and me, "Stay here until I call with an update." We were confused and worried because we didn't know what was happening. I called my cousins, they didn't know what was happening, either.

After around three hours, my stepfather came home and told us that Pap Pap had passed. I remember experiencing chest pains, crying, feeling angry, having trouble breathing, and having a lot of questions about GOD. I started to question God. Pap Pap's death was a significant event during my childhood, which I can connect to my healing journey. It was the start of my relationship with my ancestors.

The day after Pap Pap's funeral, I started to recall a male relative, a few years older than me, touching me inappropriately. We were both young at the time. It only happened once and it didn't go beyond touching. I wasn't sure of the exact age, just that it happened. When the memory surfaced, I would close my eyes and physically wave my hand across my forehead to try to forget it. I didn't want to face it.

I associated remembering that experience with Pap Pap's death and unintentionally shut off Pap Pap's memory for a while. It was just too much to deal with. I now recognize that Pap Pap's death opened a portal that I ignored. When I say a "portal," I mean that another level of consciousness had been opened for me to walk into my higher self.

Throughout my life, I had moments where I was called to my higher self, and the calling did not cease until I walked through the portal and listened to my ancestors. When Pap Pap died, the grief overwhelmed me. Outside of the grief from losing Pap Pap, I was constantly dealing with racism, and it took my focus away from recognizing the portal because I was fighting so much. I questioned if there was a GOD and if so, I asked, "Why did you take my Pap Pap?"

This time of my life was a whirlwind and a few months later, I started my period. When my cycle came, I was outside playing, which is something I did often because I was a tomboy. Out of the blue, I felt sharp pains in my stomach and back. I ran inside because I thought I had to go to the bathroom. I noticed some brown stuff in my underwear, and I called for my mom. She came in and when I explained what was happening. She said, "Oh, you got your period," with a smile.

I asked, "A period? What is that?" She explained what a period was and showed me how to use a pad. It was uncomfortable when I was on my cycle, because I had to wear that weird thing once a month.

Unfortunately, the first year proved to be the only pain-free time I had with periods. In retrospect, before Pap Pap transitioned is the last time I remember being pain-free and not dealing with the effects of endometriosis. A year after my period started, when I turned twelve, the pain started to get worse. A week before my periods, I noticed that I was spotting, I had nausea, my attitude would change, and sometimes I felt like I was going to pass out.

I remember being one of the only people in middle school who had to leave school every two weeks because I was in pain. I carried Tylenol all month, and my mom advised me to keep crackers and grapes with me to help with nausea.

On day, I was in class, and I asked the teacher to let me go to the nurse's office. She knew that I was in pain and let me leave class. I walked slowly through the halls, clutching my stomach, and when I got to the nurse's office, I told her that I had taken a Tylenol before school. As I took the bottle out of my bag, the nurse tried to stop me from taking it.

She deflected my pain and asked me, "What did you eat yesterday?" I guess she thought I was sick because I was a thick girl eating the wrong things.

As I tried to take the pill, she said, "You can't have those. You have to get them from me." I remember thinking, "I'm in so much pain just trying to walk into this office." I was frustrated and didn't understand why she was enforcing policy instead of responding to my needs. She said, "I'm going to call your mother." That was the start of medical gaslighting. I could tell she didn't care to understand my pain. I heard the nurse say, "Fawn has to leave her pills with me if she needs them in school."

I heard my mother through the receiver say, "How the hell are we supposed to know that? I gave her those pills." The nurse kept going back to the policy, and my mother asked, "Is she okay?" The next thing I knew, my mother was walking into the nurse's office. She came to that school and stood on business as she advocated for me. She  asked the nurse, "Aren't you a woman? Don't you get it?"

The nurse was trying to keep my mom calm, "Okay, you're right, she can have them. We just need to create a safety plan for her to leave them here."

Because of my painful cycles, my mom let me stay home from school. She didn't want to deal with the policies, and she wanted me to feel better. One good thing about being home was that my Granny Grace took care of me. Granny comforted me without me having to feel like I needed to be strong, and I could experience my pain. She moved in with us after Pap Pap died.

When I was sick, my Granny would make home fries, hot chocolate, and eggs. We would watch her stories, and I would sit with her while I rested with my heating pad. I grew to treasure these times with my Granny Grace.

# A CHILD NAVIGATING GYNO

# EXPERIENCES

After that, Mom took me to a gynecologist because she was fed up. She said, "These people are getting on my nerves. We gotta figure this shit out." I was so nervous to go to "that" kind of doctor, lol. But my mom was a stern advocate for me, and she taught me about advocating for myself. She taught me how to stand up for myself from the nurse to the gynecologist. Because of her, when I was 12, I was talking about safety plans and making sure to take notes whenever an adult spoke to me out of pocket.

I was a virgin, and the pap smear was extremely uncomfortable and traumatizing for me. To say it was a lot is an understatement. The doctor examined me, and my mother mentioned endometriosis because she had it. The doctor said, "She is too young to be tested for that, but birth control might help her."

The birth control helped a little after two months of using it, but that only lasted for a year and a half. During my freshman year of high school, when I was around 14, the pain grew worse again. It was as if my body adjusted itself to the medication. When I was nauseous, I felt lightheaded. I was on birth control for ten years.

At times, I would be in so much pain that I was at the point of almost passing out. My mother took me back to the gynecologist, and that doctor put me on a stronger dose of birth control. It worked sporadically. I would say that for two months, I would be fine, and for two months, I would be in pain. I noticed that movement helped, so it inspired a brief stint with basketball and track. I wasn't that good at it, lol. To me, it was a way to move and avoid the pain. Unfortunately, playing sports only led me down a difficult path of utilizing unhealthy coping mechanisms. However, I was too young to find the words to express this sentiment. I just went with it when people complimented me and said, "Fawn, I love your passion, grit, and resilience."

When I brought up my pain to anyone, the response was, "You are strong, and you will get through it. It's just a bad period." In a way, I internalized this mentality and started to believe that I was strong and resilient, and I taught myself to work through the pain. That turned out to be a double- edged sword. Grit helped me with my focus when I started to work in the movement for Black liberation and advocate for racial equity, but in the long run, it led to a health crisis.

**The Warrior is Born**

In ninth grade, I staged my first protest through menstrual pain. My Black classmates and I wanted a Black history class and a Black History Month celebration beyond learning about the same people like Martin Luther King and Rosa Parks. When we presented the idea, there was resistance from the school administrators.

On the day of the scheduled Black History program, I decided to protest and signatures on a petition. I had PMS, and the pain from my cycle was starting to brew. When I woke up for school, I took a Tylenol as a preventative measure. I packed my crackers and grapes for the nausea, and because I had already trained myself to work through the pain, "Suck it up" had become my mantra. I walked around the school with the petition that read, "Black History Class Signatures." My classmates and I stood in front of the auditorium door to block the entrance, and we asked for signatures.

When I would feel the pain, it was like an intense feeling in my stomach and lower back. The pain felt like somebody was stabbing me with a small knife. Every time I felt that pain, it made me angry. I used that feeling to drive my passion for that day and every day I advocated for something I believed in. I was already angry at the racism I was experiencing, and my physical pain gave me the language to express the anger for what I was protesting about. My pain was a physical reminder of the pain we as students were experiencing with no fucking relief. Thinking back, this experience of ignoring my pain was a tool of White supremacy. I sacrificed myself to work through pain to help my people.

Our protest, of course, upset the administration. They removed us from the assembly, took us to the office, and called my parents. When they came to pick me up, my parents looked at the administrators and said, "Good for her."

**Unhealthy Coping Skills**

My mantra of "suck it up" continued throughout high school. Advocating for fellow students is one way I coped with my physical pain. It's telling how I advocated for Black students monthly but said nothing about the monthly pain I was experiencing. The birth control, which was supposed to help with my pain, was inconsistent. I often spotted between periods, which made gym and swimming uncomfortable. The teachers and school made no accommodations for my pain.

To numb the pain, I took my first drink at the age of 10, stealing it from my parents' liquor cabinet. After that, I didn't drink again until high school. The pain became so unbearable; I would sometimes drink before school. I was a high achiever, primarily because I was always in pain, and this was how I coped. Keeping busy was a distraction, so I didn't have to feel the pain, which ultimately resulted in sleepless nights. Black women in my life reinforced this mentality and would tell me, "We all deal with it," or "Don't let them see you sweat." Another thing I heard often was, "Fake it till you make it."

At the same time, I was experiencing a lot of physical pain. I was secretly grappling with the repressed memory of being molested. It came to a head when I was

15 ½. I began having suicidal thoughts. I told my mother, and I credit her and my stepfather for creating a comfortable environment that encouraged me to speak out. I received support from them, and went to therapy.

Interestingly, my physical pain never came up during those counseling sessions. While I discussed my struggles with drinking and began to heal from those experiences and the molestation, my endometriosis remained, and I continued to deal with the effects of it.

*"Between being in college, studying, and advocating against systemic oppression, I had a lot on my plate."*

~Fawn Walker-Montgomery

# STOIC

After graduating from high school, I headed to college five hours away from home, at theee Johnson C. Smith University (JCSU). (Yes, I said theee best Historically Black College and University [HBCU]). Before leaving for school, I visited the gynecologist, who said that the pain would improve as I got older. She explained I was experiencing "bad periods." Additionally, she noted, "You have small fibroid tumors that aren't significant enough to warrant treatment."

Having that information didn't help me, especially because my pain continued to intensify. I often felt nauseous during my periods and spent a lot of time in my room seeking relief, which led me to rely heavily on pain medication. When I started college, using pain pills was like drinking water. I credit my movement work with keeping me from developing an addiction to pain pills. In addition, going to therapy for the molestation and alcohol helped as well. However, I realize that I essentially swapped one addiction for another, as my level of commitment to schoolwork and the movement for Black liberation became quite intense.

I maintained a 4.0 GPA during my Freshman year and was involved with various activities, such as peer educators. I also pledged the bestttt sorority in the world, Delta Sigma Theta Sorority, Incorporated (DST) where I led various projects. Despite my activities, I was still in pain most of the time. I managed my pain by continuing to do the work.

Around that time, my ancestors started trying to speak with me again. While I was in the process of becoming a member of DST, my Granny had a heart attack on January 1, 2000. She was in the hospital for a while, but passed a few months later, in April. I was devastated because I was so close to my Granny. Before she left, she wrote in her bible, "I will be back." I still have that note and her Bible.

I went home for the funeral, but between the pain from endo, schoolwork, trying to become a Delta, and losing my grandmother, I was numb. This got me the line name "Stoic," which means: "a person who can endure pain or hardship without showing their feelings or complaining." I remember thinking, "Wow, I have become good at hiding my pain." Once again, much like I had in high school, I took that identity and rolled with it. It was easier than focusing on endo pain, or hell, even dealing with the pain of losing my grandmother.

Navigating healthcare in college was challenging. My mother frequently advocated with the insurance company to resolve issues with medication and doctor visits. Going home during breaks became essential since the doctors at school could not treat me. One day when my period arrived, all I could manage to do was lie in bed with my heating pad, crying for several days.

That heating pad was wonderful; it's one of the best damn inventions ever. I made sure to have it with me whenever I had a bad pain day (which was often). I endured this until I was about 22. Around this time, I took a health class with an assignment focused on Black women and fibroids. While it didn't specifically mention endometriosis, it was the first time I saw myself in a medical journal. The assignment discussed the potential effects of long-term birth control on bone health.

Consequently, I decided to stop taking birth control. I became active in managing my pain. It was important to give my body a chance to heal, after years on medication. I began working out and eating better, which helped alleviate pain. However, it was challenging to maintain consistency, because, well, life happens. Between being in college, studying, and advocating against systemic oppression, I had a lot on my plate.

# ENDO CYCLE CONTINUES

After graduating with a BA in Political Science, I moved to Washington, DC. I stayed there for a year before getting pregnant at the age of 23, yet I continued to deal with my endo pain. Outside of needing my family for support, one of the reasons I came home was due to the severe pain I experienced with my periods. I knew it wasn't normal and wanted to be home if there were any issues with the pregnancy.

Thankfully, throughout my pregnancy, I didn't have a lot of pain, but I did have some spotting. It was a stressful time for me as I had to move back home and was still working and processing becoming a single parent. My daughter was born a month early and spent 12 days in the NICU. That is a pain I would not wish on anyone.

When my daughter got out of the hospital and my periods started again, the pain was horrible. I was passing out weekly and was in the ER every two days. During these visits, no one ever brought up endometriosis or any test to diagnose it. It takes some people over a year to receive a diagnosis because most doctors don't believe our pain, especially Black women. For me, the ER doctors often asked if I needed to talk with a psychologist and even mentioned if the pain was in my head. My gynecologist at the time wrote it off as fibroids because I had those too.

After months of going back and forth to the ER, my mother came to my appointment. Because she, along with my maternal aunt and a cousin, have endometriosis, she knew what to ask the doctors. Moreover, she had instructed me to take a journal to all my appointments since I was 12. At my appointments, my mother used my journal to ask questions and grill the doctor.

Due to her advocacy, I had a laparoscopic surgery at the age of 25. Medical professionals use this minimally invasive surgery to diagnose and treat endometriosis.

After my official diagnosis, you would think the doctors would focus on the endo and give me more information. However, the only thing they said was that it's bad periods that can be controlled with birth control. However, the older I got, I found out firsthand it's much more than this.

Endometriosis is a painful condition in which tissue that is similar to the inner lining of the uterus grows outside the uterus. It develops tissue that acts as the lining inside the uterus would and it thickens, breaks down and bleeds with each menstrual cycle. But it grows in places where it doesn't belong, and it doesn't leave the body (no cure). This is something that I would find out years after getting my initial diagnosis.

The years went on and I continued to experience pain and had various follow-up procedures, i.e., a dilation and curettage (D&C or DNC). A DNC is a procedure to remove tissue from inside your uterus. These procedures didn't work, so I found myself often self-advocating with my doctors for different treatments. They constantly presented two options: birth control or a hysterectomy. I was not open to having a hysterectomy in my twenties, so I said, "Oh, hell no, "I'm not doing that because I would like to get married and have more kids."

Because I didn't want to get back on the birth control pill or have a hysterectomy, I chose a birth control shot, Depo-Provera. The side effects of that medication were a little weight gain, but it was helpful, and I stayed on it for two years, with pain on and off, during this time. This pattern went on for years.

I will note that despite me going to the doctor regularly, no one mentioned that endometriosis was more than a reproductive disease or that it could spread throughout your entire body.

## Pregnancy and Racial Gaslighting

At the age of 28, I met my husband George, and we wanted to grow our family. Therefore, I got off the Depo shot, but I

*The Montgomery Family*
*George, Fawn, Grace*

couldn't get my period back. The doctors had to give me a pill for it to return. When it did, all the pain came with it. It was even worse than before. The cramps lasted the entire time I was on my period. On top of that, we were trying to get pregnant.

We tried different medical procedures to help me conceive, but they did not work. That is when I found out, after research, that infertility is connected to endometritis. I was upset, angry, and felt hopeless. Once again, I was affected by something that my medical team didn't tell me. I was surprised because I had a child but would later grow to understand that endo has 4 stages that grow worse over time. More than likely, I was in stage 2 or 3 when I got pregnant. It makes me angry and sad that the doctors didn't bother to tell me that I could possibly become infertile over time.

I went back to the gynecologist and endured more medical gaslighting. The doctors, of course, tried to make me feel like I was crazy. Telling me, "Maybe it is psychiatric or maybe it is your stomach." They would say, "You're strong." Again, hearing those words that gaslit my condition was triggering.

"No!" I told one doctor, "I know what the hell it is, it's endometriosis and you need to fix it." We went back and forth for a while because if nothing else, I'm damn sure going to advocate for myself. At my last visit with that doctor, I said, "You need to send me somewhere to somebody who knows what the hell they're doing. I have had issues with this since I was 12." Finally, he referred me to a specialist.

At that time, I was in my thirties. The new doctor recommended birth control or a surgical procedure that would cause me to never get pregnant again. Those words were devastating. I didn't want to have surgery because I didn't want to lose my ability to have children. She said, "The only thing you can do is take this birth control."

Once again, I just sucked it up and kept moving with the pain. For the next few years, I didn't take anything. I was still experiencing pain on and off, with two months of no pain and regular bleeding, or two months of intense pain. It was horrible because I also had fibroids, cysts, and benign tumors. When the pain became too much, I got back on a low dose of birth control that I stayed on for two years. I knew that the birth control could affect bones, so I didn't want to use it for too long.

## Life Kept Lifeing Through The Pain

Through the pain and advocacy with doctors, life kept lifeing. After college, I went into the human services field. Quickly I found myself getting back into old habits, specifically, using my work to distract me from my physical pain. Also, falling into the traps of white supremacy and perfectionism. This showed up as me believing that "being productive" meant working myself into exhaustion. I would work late often, go above and beyond for families, and would advocate fiercely in court.

Additionally, I was a young Black professional in Allegheny County (greater Pittsburgh). At that time, and it may still be the same, this was romanticized and tied to how well you played the game. Specifically, overworking, overachieving and being selective about what you question; to keep white people comfortable.

I never did well with games. Moreover, relationships are never sustainable. Meaning, once you do something they deem as "radical," or "scare the white people," they throw you to the side.

Therefore, I became known for being an advocate, and sort of like I had in high school, I went along with the superwoman idea of myself; managing endo pain but "pushing through." I dealt with a range of emotions. Due to the pain, I went from feeling strong to exhausted. This work ethic became my brand in my community work and lead to me becoming "hood famous" and a "community hero" at times.

*"Of my two 'handicaps' being female put*

*more obstacles in my path*

*than being black."*

~Shirley Chisolm

# BECOMING HOOD FAMOUS

My movement work started at the age of 11, in my hometown of McKeesport. It's in an area we call the Mon Valley. The valley is along the Monongahela River corridor in Allegheny County. It includes communities, such as McKeesport, Clairton, Duquesne, White Oak, Rankin, Swissvale, Braddock, North Braddock, Whitaker, Wilmerding, Homestead, West Homestead, and Munhall (to name a few).

These communities are often overlooked and routinely face challenges correlated to being under-resourced, including food insecurity, environmental justice, and community violence. They are overshadowed when it comes to the larger city of Pittsburgh. This, along with being filled with small suburbs and rural communities, makes it hard for people to accept change and push back against the racism they encounter. Each community has its own police departments, schools, and city councils. As a Councilwoman, I advocated for these communities. Along with this, I advocated for Black youth and other marginalized populations in social work. Growing up in the area, their struggles resonated with my experiences. Fighting for my community was not only a calling but it temporarily relieved the endo pain I endured.

My community work took center stage after I returned home from Washington, DC in 2002. I was 22 and eager to return home and get involved in my hometown. Unfortunately, I was met with resistance from my people, and at times, the elders. I quickly found out that some of them wanted to focus on having White proximity, to maintain self-preservation for their families, rather than seek justice.

Additionally, I grappled internally with navigating a spectrum of approaches to my advocacy, going between the philosophies of Martin Luther King, Jr. and Malcolm X. I had community elders tell me to watch how I said things, and police my organizing style. They would often see me as a villain because I was radical, and to them, not safe. They would mention things like, "You'll scare the White people." It surprised me that my words and actions were sometimes met with more criticism than the oppressive system itself.

I'd respond to my elders, "I am not the problem; I am responding to the system with my actions, but what the system is doing to us is killing us." I would often ask them, "Why is the energy towards me and not towards our oppressors?" Often, there was no response. I frequently received advice that I needed to learn how to "play the game." I instinctively resisted, recognizing that no amount of strategic maneuvering or personal achievements could shield me from the realities of racism.

Despite this, I pressed on and created my own spaces. For me, it was important to establish these spaces so that those who come behind me don't have to endure some of the challenges I faced. I wanted to pass the torch and ensure that others wouldn't have to fight, as I did.

## McKeesport City Council

Therefore, in 2008, I successfully ran for McKeesport City Council. I was elected as one of the youngest council members in my community under the age of 30. In addition, in 2016, I was the first Black person to run for state representative in my community. Yes, the first. Subsequently, I became a trailblazer in many respects. While this may seem like a commendable accomplishment, it ultimately led to feelings of anxiety, burnout, and health issues.

I did eight years on council. I say "did" because I experienced a range of emotions, from excitement to anger while serving. I was the only person on Council with views centered on community, Black liberation, and social change. This didn't make me friends and often resulted in my colleagues responding negatively to my feedback. While on council I held a full-time job at a local Black social services nonprofit, where I encountered pressure to chase "Black excellence" and perfectionism.

## Panic Attacks

I remember my supervisor saying, "Real leaders don't get overwhelmed." Although I was taught to respect my elders, I was also groomed to challenge systems that didn't serve me or my community. Due to this and my battles on council, I leaned more toward individualism, as I was often advocating alone.

I started to experience panic attacks from stress. I'd have one before I spoke at a City Council meeting, and sometimes before I had to facilitate a meeting at work. My chest would tighten up, I would have trouble breathing, and my negative self-talk would be loud in my ears and heart. I would think things like, "Girl, nobody will listen to you. Why are you wasting your time?"

I knew that when I spoke up and spoke out at

work and on council, there was a consequence. It wasn't just going to be backlash for me because I have a family. The stress of my work affected my relationship with them as well. Moreover, the anxiety of my resistance caused my endometriosis to spread as a result of my stress.

Close to the time of a council meeting, I'd think about the negative statements of my colleagues, such as, "You're not smart enough, you don't know what you're talking about. That's not how things work around here." Or "Not everything is about race, I don't see color."

Because I had a background in therapy, I knew exactly what was happening to me and I blew it off for a couple of weeks. One day George came home early from work and walked in on me in the middle of a panic attack. I had been paying bills and thinking that he and my daughter wouldn't be home for a while. I sat on the floor and let it all go. "Damn, I gotta deal with the Council meeting tomorrow, I gotta pay these bills. I gotta ." In that moment, I had a lot of racing thoughts about what I had to do and what I had to deal with.

I put my hand on my chest, started gasping for air, and I started to sob. To my surprise, I heard the door open then George came into the house, but I couldn't pull myself together. He immediately bent down and sat next to me. Out of concern, he fired questions at me.

"Did someone break in?" He looked around and noticed that the floor was in disarray. "What's going on with you?"

I said, "I'm having a panic attack."

I couldn't hide it from him anymore. I was secretly relieved he had come home. "When did you start having these panic attacks, Fawn?"

"About a month ago." In that moment, I let my guard down and the performative strong Black woman act. I think that is one of the first times George really saw me cry.

George said, "We need to pray together before you do the bills, or before you experience something you feel will cause you to have this response." He grabbed my hand and prayed for me. That started our ritual of praying together before any major event.

A lot of this was because I was maintaining the "strong Black woman" image I adopted way back, when I was in middle school. Wearing this mask of being strong, while suffering, was my façade. It was further emphasized in how I acted out my duties as a McKeesport Councilwoman. I often felt like the Mayor and went to various events, spoke, helped, and often traveled to other parts of the county. While doing this, I was advocating for people, and I didn't gain a lot of friends.

At times, the City Council meetings were like being in an odd, and at times, abusive relationship. What I mean is that as a Black woman, everything I said was met with aggression. Of course, I stood up for myself, yet

I often felt like I was on a hamster wheel running fast to fight for people who didn't want my help. My husband had to attend a lot of these meetings to protect me. If he couldn't be present, he'd send someone. This helped and they started to "back off" (at least in the public anyway).

During these times, I would often read quotes and books about my ancestors who endured so much, so I could be on Council. People such as Shirley Chilsom, who said she had "two handicaps" of being a woman and Black person. I got to see the true meaning of this quote being on the Council. Also, Harriett Tubman, who fought and risked her own life to get our people to freedom. Connecting with my ancestors helped me stay in the fight.

*"I think we are all born to make*

*our mark in the world."*

~Roxanne Shanté, Hip Hop Artist

# POLITICS AND COMMUNITY WORK

As my first term on McKeesport Council ended, I found myself in a heated battle while seeking my second term. My team and I knocked on over 500 doors, made over 200 calls, and ran a true grassroots campaign. My colleagues were upset that I was vocal and questioned the votes. They didn't want me to win, so they selected opponents to run against me. I remember on election day I was behind twenty votes. The next morning, I was in the lead with nine votes. This led to them challenging votes, and we had to wait two weeks for the results.

It was hard to go to the grocery store; everyone asked me for updates that I didn't have. In the end, I was ahead with three votes and won the election. This is one reason I tell people to vote, especially in local races.

During this time, I also ran for State Representative twice amidst death threats and my name being slandered. I did nothing to deserve this treatment, except to be a Black woman who fought for change. These challenges became a lot for me to handle, as most of the commentary took place in our local media. I remember thinking, "Is it worth it to, in a way, put history on my back?" I am thankful for my ancestors, family, and close friends who kept me grounded during these times.

Running for the state seats led to party switching. I didn't have switching to being a Republican on my bingo card. While I didn't share their values, it was a means to an end, a sort of "the enemy of my enemy's" that comes from Sun Tzu's The Art of War. The issue of dealing with the dangling of diversity, that sometimes exists within the Democratic Party, played a huge part in this. Specifically, having diversity programs that promote Black people running for office but, never giving them resources to win and run campaigns that can compete.

When I did start to ask some of the committee members for their support, I was met with racist names and shady deals when I was trying to get my name on the ballot as a Democrat. No Black person had ever run for a state seat in the Mon Valley, so it was met with heavy resistance. The thought of another Black woman going through this kept me in the fight. I recognize you can't have a second without a first.

I will never forget when they took me to court to get my name off the ballot. My campaign ran a write-in and won to get my name back on. I didn't win the state elections, but I did get more than 60% of the community vote. More importantly, I opened the door for another Black woman, Summer Lee, to run. She became an amazing Congresswoman, supporter, and comrade in the movement. From there, I ran for Mayor of McKeesport, but didn't win. Losing this as well as the State Rep. races was heartbreaking for me, and I remember thinking will these folks ever be ready for change? And will I even live to see it. The heartbreak I felt from my community was even more than any relationship I had.

I took some time off after this and leaned into my consulting and work with my team at Take Action Advocacy Group (TAAG), formerly known as Take Action Mon Valley (TAMV).

TAAG is a labor of love for me, and in many ways; it helped me to break out of my individualism. Activism is a thankless job, often met with criticism. Outside of my kitchen table, my husband, Mother, daughter, and close friends, support was hard to receive. At times, I had to work in a silo to protect myself. TAAG allowed me to see the power of community.

Because I was an elected official for the City of McKeesport, when the community came to me about starting a community group, I listened. My cousin, Mae Herriott Hudson had just lost her son Carlos Hudson. He lost his life along with Jana Randolph due to gun violence. Mae attended a meeting in Pittsburgh about the lack of homicides of Black people being solved in Pittsburgh. She wanted to have a group to address these problems in the Mon Valley.

After the initial meeting, we convened several follow-up sessions where I conducted a SWOT analysis and developed community action plans. I noticed that people came from all over the Mon Valley, and this led us

*Logo Design, Soleil Meade*

to name ourselves Take Action Mon Valley (TAMV).

At this time, TAAG was a community group, and no one was getting paid. We inspired a movement for social justice and Black liberation in our communities. A few of my team members at TAAG also ran for office in McKeesport and Duquesne. For instance, one person became a member of the McKeesport School Board, while another ran for the McKeesport City Council. Additionally, two individuals ran in Duquesne, with one winning a Council seat and Nickole Nesby made history as the first Black woman to become Mayor.

This involvement in local politics and organizing garnered me "hood fame." This, along with having a deep connection to my community, is something I was and continue to be proud of. At this time, although TAAG experienced a lot of growth, simultaneously, I started experiencing misogyny in politics and local organizing.

## Black Misogyny

Black women are sometimes separated from the cause due to misogyny. I, too, have experienced being overlooked, ignored, or erased because I am deemed "too strong," or "not submissive" enough. This toxicity was wild for me because I was fighting against racism and police violence IN the struggle with Black men. At times, I was also in a principled struggle with my Black comrades who identified as men, over their misogyny and sexism. This is not new and something that our elders dealt with.

One of the most well-known examples of this is the Combahee River Collective statement. The collective was a group of Black feminists who developed a document in the 70's that stated their objections to not feeling a part of white feminism, and at times turned away from the Black liberation movement due to patriarchy. Their work remains true until this day and was pivotal in Black feminism.

Unfortunately, the effects of patriarchy continued to affect me. This is something I noticed from a young age. I saw it in **rap (yes, I say rap and not hip hop, lol)** and in my community. Some suggest this began in the 1980s with gangster rap, but as someone born in 1980, I remember witnessing the effects of misogyny and exploitation much earlier. For example, in the UTFO song "Roxanne, Roxanne," the group describes catcalling, and it reminds me of my experiences of being catcalled at the age of ten.

The song in a way helped to normalize misogyny. It describes a group of men catcalling a woman consistently. When Roxanne Shante responded to UTFO in her song, *"Roxanne's Revenge,"* she was only fourteen years old; it was my first memory of Black feminism. It may sound surprising, but for a Black woman to speak truth to power at that time was incredibly powerful. One of the lyrics that stands out to me is:

*He said, "You call yourself an MC?"*

*I said, "This is true,"*

*He said, "Explain to me really what MCs must do."*

*I said, "Listen very close cause I don't say this every*

*day . . ."*

The acceptance and normalization of patriarchy is connected to how it manifests in our communities and Black liberation spaces. Specifically, in the hood, with the actions of older men parking across the street from a school and making comments to young Black girls as they leave. This includes whistling, buying gifts, giving them money, and openly discussing how they are waiting until the girls turn 18. It's important to acknowledge that older Black women often put Black boys in similar situations.

Growing up I was and still am a thick girl (think thighs save lives, lol). When I was in middle school, at times, it was hard to walk home from school when older men, young men, and older women pointed out my hips and thighs. Some of my aunts would mention how "thick" I was getting, which was annoying, as if I had control over it. This is something that happens today. Let me add that as a thick Black girl, we don't need reminders about our body shape.

Throughout this, I continued to suffer from endometriosis pain and noticed the effects it had on my physical and mental health. I realized that, to heal, I had to unlearn my relationship with white supremacy; and how I internalized these principles in my life.

# UNLEARNING WHITE SUPREMACY

At times, Black people internalize white supremacy without even knowing it. Particularly, with perfectionism, urgency, internalized racism, defensiveness, quantity over quality, capitalism, keeping white people comfortable (white proximity), worship of the written word, paternalism, either-or thinking, power hoarding, fear of open conflict, and individualism. I mentioned how individualism, misogyny and perfectionism affected me in prior sections of this book.

Specifically, this was highlighted when I discussed my first term on the McKeesport Council, which was marked by solo advocacy for racial justice (individualism). This also shows up when I described the impact of Black masculinity on my experiences as an activist, in the movement for Black liberation. Furthermore, Black excellence and perfectionism was addressed when I discussed the pressures I encountered in my former job.

Other ways this manifested was me ignoring pain and continuing to work. I would often be in the streets organizing, while in pain. Sacrificing myself to do the "work" and practicing internalized ableism. This occurs when one absorbs negative beliefs about themselves and their disability. For me, this was connected to how I internalized white supremacy with the belief that my worth was tied to productivity.

I often rejected my pain and bought into unrealistic views of perfection. Moreover, that my worth was in what I did for my people and not just for being "FAWN." I had to do the work to unlearn these behaviors to heal. Recognizing this truth was crucial, especially considering challenges within my community.

Those challenges were rotted in "racism," a theme throughout the book. Where I live has had an impact on my mental and physical health. This is true for other Black women, too. These concerns were highlighted in the City of Pittsburgh's Gender Equity report in 2019. It stated that this region is one of the worst for Black women to live, citing disparities in Black maternal health, jobs, and other health disparities.

I have witnessed locally what stress, and burnout can do to Black women. Many Black women have died fighting, and I didn't want that to become my story! While going along on this journey, I discovered how much self-reflection goes into unlearning white supremacy.

**Unlearning Is a Lifelong Journey**

White supremacy is much more than the KKK attacking Black people. It's an ideology that is embedded in our society through direct and indirect (subtle) biases built into our institutions. This starts as early as elementary school with policing our hairstyles and clothing, and it continues into adulthood at work.

The process of unlearning starts with making a personal inventory of the ways you notice yourself engaging in these behaviors. Since we are not a monolith, this will look different for everyone. Some other ways this came up for me was with worship of the written word and urgency. This shows up in various ways, specifically through the belief that unless you have correct documentation, grammar, and strong writing skills, some white people won't take you seriously. There is an expectation that everything has to be done following a certain writing style, like the American Psychological Association (APA).

As a writer, this is something I have dealt with. I had to recognize that I had a "white gaze" in my writing. For me, this came from Black people overly criticizing my writing, especially in my twenties and thirties, as a young Black professional, new to the workforce. I didn't have the language for it then, but now I understand that they were overly focusing on only the white readers who may read or judge it.

I was constantly gaslighted about this. People would text me when I posted on social media and mention I forgot a comma, period, or misspelled two words. I was often told I couldn't write how I talk or express everything I felt. "Fawn, you can't write things like this; it'll scare white people, or no one will take you seriously." Some said, "You sound so radical and angry."

I remember thinking, "Ok, thanks for the feedback, but what about what I said?"

The anxiety of worrying about grammar and writing things "perfectly" became a lot. I was always conscious about how people would view my grammar, not what I was writing. It affected my ability to imagine and be creative. I stopped writing altogether for a few years. It wasn't until I started to unlearn white supremacy that I started writing again in 2021. Despite this, it still affects my writing, as unlearning is a lifelong process.

Worship of the written word connects to how the

Bible and Christianity are at times utilized to pacify Black people and stop us from resisting. The Bible has at times been utilized to reinforce this and persuade Black people to forgive rather than fight. This began during slavery and has persisted in schools and churches. Bible verses such as "turn the other cheek" are used to quiet justified rage born from the brutality of enslavement.

In earlier chapters, I spoke about dealing with this from our elders. My organizing style was criticized, and I had the now-infamous quote by our forever First Lady Michelle Obama, "When they go low, we go high," thrown in my face. This creates respectability politics and division between those who "put up with indirect and direct racism" to get by, and those who realize that we no longer need to do so. I often want to scream to tell some of our elders, "While I understand why you did that, we no longer have to do it!"

Additionally, some politicians also use this to

encourage Black Christians to adopt a colonized perspective on the Black LGBTQ+ community, specifically Black transwomen, at times, causing a strained relationship resulting in "church hurt" and trauma. Before I continue, I think it's important to note that my intention is not to criticize Christianity. My hope is to address this topic and help you understand how white supremacy, embedded in Christianity, impacted my wellness journey and Black people's view of ourselves and our ancestors.

At one time, I identified as a Christian, and many of my loved ones remain connected to both Christianity and the Bible. Neither of which is wrong. However, after taking steps to deconstruct my internalized perceptions of white supremacy, I unlocked a new level of consciousness. This process led me to hold Christianity accountable for its role in perpetuating white supremacy.

After reading and studying our history, I begin to

recognize that many of our ancestors practiced and assimilated into Christianity out of survival. Before we were kidnapped and forced into slavery, Black people practiced various forms of African spirituality. Some of our ancestors held onto their spiritual beliefs as a form of resistance. They utilized breathing, plants, and water to connect with nature and to heal. Their resilience in maintaining these traditions emphasizes the importance of reconnecting with them. I know "resilience" has become a buzzword, but that's because of the white gaze that has sometimes become associated with it. Despite this, we must reclaim our language and other practices.

Contrary to what we've been taught, yoga, meditation, hiking, gardening, and growing food are not "white people things;" they are valuable traditions passed down from our ancestors. To get to this, I had to unlearn co-opted truths and reclaim my true spiritual practices. This involved accepting the historical framework of why these practices were hidden from us and understanding their importance in our collective liberation.

I didn't realize it at the time, but unlearning my previous beliefs and being open my roots of African spiritual practices led me to save my own life and heal myself. It provided me with a blank canvas that I could fill with the voices of my ancestors, a process that came to a head during the racial justice uprisings.

*"I found it hard to breathe . . ."*

~Fawn Walker-Montgomery

# THE BODY KEEPS SCORE: I'M MORE THAN LABOR

I started to notice that my pain was getting worse. In 2020, all of this came to a head. Like so many other community organizers, I was heavily involved with the uprisings and engaged in voter outreach for the election. In addition, the weight of working with various families who had lost loved ones to the police, took a toll on me. I started to disassociate when I spoke to them, it was like I was having out of body experiences.

I remember that I would go to a quiet place by water. It was a lot to take in and the trauma was piling up. I am in no way saying that this even compares to the pain they were experiencing, I am just sharing my experiences. While this is the most rewarding work I have ever done, it did affect my mental health. Additionally, endometriosis was still causing me pain, and during this time, I was frequently traveling to doctors about my stomach issues. I was diagnosed with irritable bowel syndrome (IBS), diverticulitis, and gastritis.

It seemed that no amount of medicine or pills were working for me. After the election, I was diagnosed with COVID-19, which turned into long COVID coupled with pneumonia. It affected my lungs and heart. This made it very difficult to protest and, at times, even to walk.

I found it hard to breathe and became winded just walking up the stairs. When I was diagnosed in the ER, they told me that my oxygen was low and that blood was not flowing through my heart valve quickly enough. They recommended new medication, or I might have to be placed on a ventilator due to damage to my lungs and heart. I felt numb. Less than 72 hours prior, I had been at a protest, and now I was fighting for my life, faced with the decision of whether to take a new drug from a system I didn't trust.

I have never been one to get excited about new drugs or vaccinations, given the medical history of racism in this country. After much consideration, I decided to take the medication. It helped, and after a week, I was released from the hospital with orders to rest at home.

I remember noticing that the calls, texts, and emails stopped coming because I wasn't doing anything or producing labor for the movement. I could count on one hand how many people called to see if I was ok. I thought to myself, "If I die today, folks will say, "Fawn really cared about the movement, she was a great advocate for Black people and the Mon Valley." However, they wouldn't say that I cared about FAWN that I took care of myself.

More importantly, my daughter and the other Black girls who looked up to me would think we are only good for our labor. I had to realize that most of my relationships were tied to my labor. This realization allowed me to do something I hadn't done in a while: REST. I went to physical therapy for my lungs and found a cardiologist for my heart. This, along with the work I have done in unlearning, prepared me for my hardest battle with endometriosis to come.

**Pain, Forgiving Myself and Loss**

In November of 2021, I got a pain in my side and stomach that did not leave until July 2022. It was a sharp, dull, numbing pain in my lower abdomen. TAAG was having an event, and the pain came that morning. I took some Tylenol, but nothing worked. I did the event with my team and went to the hospital later.

They immediately said it was diverticulitis and possibly a gallbladder issue. I got Dilaudid for the pain, but this made me vomit. The tests came back negative for the gallbladder and diverticulitis. ALL of the tests came back with no issues. They attempted to tell me that it might be in my head. To avoid more medical gaslighting, I left and went home.

The visits to emergency rooms became a weekly occurrence. This was happening around my daughter's birthday and her senior year. I was determined to try to "be present" for her. It broke my heart to spend the morning of her birthday in the hospital.

The pain started to move throughout my body. It went from my stomach to my legs, hips, back, and sides. It was still sharp, and I began to believe that I was dying because the pain was constant. I started to plan for death and was suicidal. Often going over my will and writing down my passwords for my family to find.

I went to all the doctors you could think of, gynecologists, gastroenterologists, etc. They were all unable to give me any answers. During this period, I spent a lot of time with myself doing self-reflection. I battled feelings of guilt about not slowing down sooner to realize something was off. I went through a range of emotions, from anger to sadness to rage. I also felt like "someone" was trying to tell me something. This someone seemed bigger than a person. I would later discover this was the spirit nudging me to continue to rest and go through a process of forgiving myself. This was instrumental in giving me the hope I needed to fight for my life.

I got a Black therapist who has been instrumental in my healing. This was the first time in my life I had a Black therapist, and it was extremely helpful in my unlearning of white supremacy. I was able to speak freely to someone who understood me, without having to explain myself.

In addition, I hired a self-care coach, Candice Denise, who is my classmate from JCSU. As my self-care coach, Candace has helped me to see that self-care is way more than just taking vacations. I realized that therapy and self-care are medicine. They are both necessary for my healing journey.

Moreover, Tricia Hershey's book *Rest Is Resistance* was also helpful in this process. It helped me see how white supremacy contributed to my equating productivity with self-worth. One quote that stands out to me is: "Along with stealing your imagination and time, grind culture has stolen the ability for pleasure, hobbies, leisure, and experimentation."

We are caught up in a never-ending cycle of going and doing. It's wild to admit, but in 2021, I daydreamed for the first time in a while. I spent over 30 years fighting white supremacy, never stopping to imagine or dream about anything. Another piece of this is how I learned to start feeling things.

**Loss Continues: Feeling All The Things**

For so long, I never stopped to feel. I didn't slow down long enough to feel ANYTHING. This is both because the shit hurt with the endo and dealing with the trauma of racism. I often got death threats from doing the work and have lost relationships with close family members. For instance, the relationship between me and my stepfather is strained.

He's a cop for our local police department. You can imagine how this may cause some issues, with my movement work. What's ironic is that he was instrumental in radicalizing me; and now we barely talk. There was no huge argument, he just didn't like my new abolition views and decided to distance himself. Growing up he, Pap Pap and my Uncle Daryl (who has now become an ancestor) were the closest things I had to a Father figure. So, losing that for simply advocating for my community was a lot for me to FEEL.

My therapist helped me to come to terms with this and in some respects "mourn" this separation. If it's in the will of the Most High and ancestors we will speak again one day, if not, I'm okay, knowing I'm advocating for what is right and I am honoring my TRUE SELF.

Therapy and working with my self-care coach has helped me to find courage to fight for my life. I utilized the internet to look up my symptoms and YouTube to watch videos of women with similar pain. I didn't have to research for hours to make it count. Their descriptions of their pain helped me to see that this might be my endometriosis or fibroids. I had both, but I was confused because the pain wasn't just in my womb area.

Although doctors had theories and ideas about my health, I knew that there was something deeper and ultimately, I know my body. That led me to schedule a gynecologist's appointment. I trusted that spirit was leading me to understand my endo journey even more.

*My biggest takeaway from this time was realizing I am more than my labor, and I won't die fighting white supremacy!*

~Fawn Walker-Montgomery

# MEDICAL ADVOCACY AND STAGE 4 ENDOMETRIOSIS

During the visit, I faced yet another battle with medical gaslighting. The doctor attempted to convince me that I had a UTI. She implied that my husband had cheated on me and could have given me an STD! "Lady," I told her, "My husband didn't cheat on me, and I don't have no damn STD, something else is wrong." I insisted on a sonogram, which revealed that my fibroid had grown and that I had cysts as well. She recommended that, despite the pain, they were not at a size that warranted removal, she suggested I take birth control and wait until after her maternity leave to schedule surgery.

Needless to say, this did not sit well with me. I asked her if she would want to wait for relief if she were in pain. Oddly enough, the gynecologists and emergency room doctors never even mentioned my endometriosis, despite it being diagnosed at the age of 25 and noted in my medical records. After advocating for myself, she provided me with names of a few surgeons who specialized in endometriosis.

I called all of them but found that they were booked for six months. I then called back to obtain more names and went through that list. I remember feeling frustrated that I was never informed about endometriosis specialists. Eventually, I secured an appointment, but it was two months out. At times, I felt like I either wanted to fight or just give up. During those moments, I would often feel a spirit guiding me to rest and breathe.

In these quiet times of rest, I would read medical journals. One day, I read a medical journal article detailing bladder issues in women with endometriosis, which prompted me to make an appointment with a urologist. The doctor informed me that I had pelvic muscle spasms. Yes, you read that correctly, I was experiencing spasms in or near my vagina. She explained that stress, along with the endometriosis caused it.

To help with this, I saw a pelvic floor physical therapist, which proved extremely beneficial for both my physical and mental health. Initially, the experience felt "weird" for me. This type of therapy involves internal work, where the therapist uses their finger inside the vagina to perform some massage and breath exercises. Although it felt odd at first, it ultimately helped. They took the time to explain my pain, where it was occurring, and how to address it.

A few weeks after starting therapy, I finally saw the endometriosis specialist who confirmed the diagnosis. He informed me that the endometriosis had spread throughout my entire body and affected my bladder and rectum. Additionally, he stated I had stage 4 endometriosis and would need a full hysterectomy to remove it. I finally had an answer, which led to a whirlwind of emotions.

I was furious that no one, including previous doctors, had ever told me that this was a full-body disease. I had no idea it could spread this way. I had various thoughts racing through my mind, such as, "Do I even have diverticulitis? Why wouldn't anyone bring this up?" I had worked hard to advocate for an early diagnosis, and now I was facing the prospect of a hysterectomy.

At 42, I had to prepare for the removal of my uterus. However, they couldn't schedule the surgery at that appointment, and I had to wait for the scheduler to call me. They prescribed me Lupron to stop my period and the estrogen that fuels the growth of endometriosis. When you have a period, estrogen increases, so the medication was intended to help. One side effect of the drug was putting me into early menopause.

Despite this, I finally had an answer, which was somewhat enough to push me to keep fighting. My biggest takeaway from this time was realizing I am more than my labor, and I won't die fighting white supremacy!

## CBD and Life-Threatening Hysterectomy

It took weeks to schedule the surgery. I called and messaged in the medical communication system every two days. During this time, the pain consistently went from an 8 to a 10. The pelvic floor therapy and Lupron only dented the pain.

I remember crying weekly in front of my daughter. For me, this was different because I had just started to cry and let myself feel things, something I worked on in therapy. Crying in front of my daughter, I think, helped us grow closer, as she saw me as a person in pain and not just her mother who always "gets it done" and powers through the pain.

One day, my husband recommended using CBD. He had long been using holistic methods of growing food to heal from diabetes. Since my endometriosis had spread and was in my pelvic area, the CBD helped to loosen the pelvic muscles and relax my body. I mentioned before that this was the time of my daughter's senior year in high school. CBD was instrumental in helping me be a part of her celebrations, even though I was in horrible pain. It also helped me to stop taking over-the-counter pills.

I was taking 8-10 Tylenol a day with no relief. The morphine they give in the ER didn't help either. Tylenol can at times do more harm than good. At times, it can cause liver damage, bleeding in the upper gastrointestinal tract, and hypertension. Naturally, I was grateful for a holistic approach to counter long-term effects of prescription medication.

I should mention that when I started to use CBD, I had to get over my thinking about it, i.e., unlearn. What I mean is that we are taught that marijuana is bad. It's been labeled illegal and used to put Black people in jail unjustly. Additionally, it's now being sold as a treatment and a way to make money. At the same time, Black people remain incarcerated for doing what some in power now consider as a medical treatment. White people, specifically White women, have taken it and used it for their wellness.

Marijuana also has a long history with African and Indigenous cultures. They would often utilize it as herbal medicine. It comes from the earth, and our ancestors, yet we have been criminalized for use as a part of systematic racism. This is important because while I am fighting endo internally, I continue to deal with racism externally. This is something that many Black women who are suffering from endo can relate to. I would often feel exhausted with the realization that I had to advocate for my life to survive with endo and against the effects racism. Having to advocate at every walk of life, including with doctors, is common for Black women.

The racial medical gaslighting showed up a lot during doctor's appointments and while advocating for justice in local communities. If I had to describe medical gaslighting, I would say it's like a mixture of micro and macro aggressions. Some doctors, nurses, and other medical professionals may not intend to do this but, they let their bias and stereotypical views of the "strong Black woman" dictate how they give medical advice.

When I decided to run for office and become a community leader, I accepted the fact that at times I would have to be a public person. This, at times, led to me being on TV fighting for justice and liberation. Therefore, doctors would often say, "I see you on the news fighting, I know you, you're strong enough to take this." On top of that, I was still in the movement and fighting for racial justice. While I had taken a significant step back, I was still doing some things part-time. I still had to work my fulltime job to maintain health insurance and to live. As a result, I was still organizing around police and environmental justice issues such as clean air, water, and access to adequate medical care. The CBD helped, it gave me the strength to do these things. I believe it should be studied as a treatment for endo.

After three weeks, my hysterectomy was finally scheduled. I was nervous because of the risks involved, especially since endometriosis had spread to my rectum. There was a possibility something could go wrong, and I could end up having to wear a colostomy bag.

On the day of the procedure, my mother and husband went with me. The surgery was supposed to take 2 to 4 hours, but it ended up lasting seven hours. When I woke up, I saw my husband and heard the nurses whispering, "Oh no, I hope she's okay. Poor thing." I felt sore and asked my husband, "What the hell happened?"

He explained that the surgery took seven hours. The doctor then came in and explained the surgery to me, "Your endometriosis was one of the worst cases I have seen. There were layers and layers of lesions and scar tissue that needed to be removed."

Some of this tissue was on my bladder, and during the procedure, the doctors had invertedly nicked the ureter, which meant I had to wear a catheter for 2 to 3 weeks until it healed. Also, an abscess exploded in my stomach (almost killing me). This then turned the procedure into an emergency, and they had to call in a urologist to repair the damage.

I was in shock but relieved to be alive. I stayed in the hospital for a week. While there, I did a video blog and came to terms with some truths. The idea for the blog came a few days before the surgery. After deciding to fight for my life and to use advocacy to help others do the same, I started a video blog on YouTube.

This was new to me, I was not accustomed to vulnerability. In the blog, I shared some hard truths, specifically that a hysterectomy is not a cure for endometriosis, as there is no definitive cure. I recognized the possibility that endometriosis could return.

Additionally, despite my advocacy I did all the research on endo and asked various questions; no doctors had ever informed me that endometriosis could spread. I also had to forgive myself for not recognizing that something was off. Furthermore, I emphasized that endometriosis is one of the most under-researched diseases. Despite all the scans I had undergone, it didn't show up on any of them. Accepting these truths was the first step towards me coming into my higher self.

*" . . . the reason I was now using these methods was that I had magic inside of me and the power to heal myself."*

~Fawn Walker-Montgomery

# EMBRACING THE JOURNEY TO MY HIGHER SELF

Throughout the book, I have mentioned the need to unlearn white supremacy, as well as the significance of spirit and ancestors. After the surgery, all of these elements came to a head, and I began to see how they were interconnected. For example, I had to unlearn how my relationship with white supremacy had affected my decisions, views of myself, and my understanding of rest.

Even though I had a self-care coach explain to me that the idea of true rest went beyond spa trips, this is the first time I embraced it, 6 or 7 months later. A few months after the surgery I had the opportunity to put this into practice by doing a rest retreat with the Windcall Institute. The organization guides long-time organizers in transformative practices. I was chosen to go on a three-week sabbatical in New Mexico. Here, we would have no schedule, no work, and no plans, just a quiet ranch with a bed and food. This was the first time I would not be working for such a long period. I knew that if I had not done the work to unlearn, I would never have done something like this.

It was truly transformative for me. I had the pleasure of connecting with other movement organizers, going on my first hike, learning how to make fires, and trying different foods. In the past, I thought these activities were just "white people things." Before the end of the trip, I was going on hikes alone and even did a solo hike of the Bandelier National Monument.

During the retreat one of my close comrades in the movement, Celeste Scott, passed away. My heart was broken for her family and community. When I say family, I mean the chosen and unchosen ones. I had become a part of the chosen family.

She was a fierce advocate who will be missed. I almost left the retreat but, stayed after friends reminded me that this is what she would have wanted. I still felt all 'the things': feeling bad; and having 'survivor's guilt.' So, many Black women have died fighting for our people. I thought, "what made me any different?" While also feeling relieved that I was finally resting. I was also sad and often thought about her son. This was during the time that the new Black Panther was released, after Chadwick passed and went on to become an ancestor. I went to see it with my comrades at the retreat and cried for hours at the end of the movie. I appreciated them for letting me have that moment.

All of this opened me up to being guided by the spirit of the Most High and my ancestors, consistently receiving messages to rest and breathe. Rest played a crucial role in my self-reflection and in beginning to practice self-love. It also provided me with the space to conduct medical research and listen to my ancestors. This ultimately led me to a pelvic floor therapist, who informed me that breathing exercises could be a treatment for pelvic pain and endometriosis. So, when I kept receiving the message to rest and breathe, I realized those were whispers from my ancestors. Additionally, a few weeks after the surgery and the removal of the catheter, my pain decreased to a level of 3-4. Although I started to feel better, I still sensed that something was off and didn't feel like myself. I felt like someone was trying to tell me something.

During this time, the pain had decreased significantly but was still present, as there is no cure for endometriosis. I had completely stopped taking Tylenol and other over-the-counter medications. Instead, I utilized breathing, movement, baths, heat and CBD to manage pain.

One day, while sitting on the couch, I received a download: the reason I was now using these methods was that I had magic inside of me and the power to heal myself. I also realized that our ancestors used these practices during slavery. This prompted me to begin researching what this meant. I felt confused because I kept hearing the question, "Are you a witch?" After doing some reading, I discovered that the ancestors were trying to tell me about hoodoo.

Hoodoo is an African derived practice that deals with everyday concerns using herbs. In addition, it uses the natural elements of water, air, fire, and the earth (earthly magic). It's the result of people who faced unimaginable suffering but, refused to give up. Hoodoo offers the ability to act on racial justice, which at times can be challenging to address due to lived trauma.

After our ancestors were kidnapped, they wanted to hold onto some form of their practices. Therefore, they practice this but hid it in plain sight. It was hidden in their rituals, prayers, food, water, air, and sacred objects. They utilized these things to seek protection, healing, and justice. These practices were preserved through oral tradition, passed down within families and communities. They also incorporated elements of Christianity; the preferred religion that slaves were forced to practice. This integration is evident in aspects such as renaming spirit possessions as "catching the holy spirit" and replacing African incantations with Bible verses.

One major part of hoodoo is having a deep connection with your ancestors. This is another thing that I received over the years. I remember always feeling connected to my maternal grandmother and movement ancestors, feeling like they were always with me and would take over when I needed to fight for justice. So, for me, it was fitting that I was recognizing that this is the message I was trying to hear. During the surgery, when I almost died, a symbolic portal opened, and I walked through it. I believe I ignored these signs in the past; I was busy fighting white supremacy.

Having this download come through at this time was helpful for my mental health as well. I was struggling with almost dying during the surgery. It's odd to think that if I would have not advocated for myself, I may be dead. This connection helped me to process this. To learn more about Hoodoo, I continued to conduct research and my connection grew stronger.

**Practicing Hoodoo With Ancestral Veneration**

My research included connecting with and being part of a community. Through my unlearning, I grew to understand the power of collective healing. My experience at Windcall also contributed to this. I met people there who were able to guide me to my spiritual mentor, Shana Nunnelly, a Hoodoo priestess and sound healer. She taught me the basics of Hoodoo and guided me through steps in using this to heal myself.

Ancestral veneration is the practice of honoring one's ancestors and the roles they play in the daily lives of the living. It's about honoring your ancestors, not worshiping them. It's about holding space for, and respecting those in your blood line and heritage.

When we venerate our ancestors, we're keeping their stories alive. Black people have a deep connection to our ancestors due to the trauma of slavery and racism. They endured so much so we could survive. Due to this they deserve our honor and respect.

For me, this process started when I took a course on genealogy. Here I had the opportunity to conduct family research and have my African ancestry completed. I started talking with my oldest living relatives, on my mother's side. I learned some things that contributed to my healing.

For example, through African ancestry, I was able to discover that we originated from the Tikar tribe of Cameroon. We were sold along the Atlantic slave trade and ended up living in Sumter, South Carolina.

My grandmother, Grace Herriott Lloyd's father, Charles Herriott grew up there, and her mother, Helen Savage, was from Baltimore, MD. Great Grandpa Herriott stayed in the south until he encountered a racially traumatic experience with racism. He was walking down the street and was told to move out of the way for a white woman. After refusing, he was sentenced to work on the chain gang. Upon his release, Great Grandpa Herriot left South Carolina and vowed never to go back or take his kids down there. They moved north to McKeesport, PA for work at the steel mill and to escape the trauma of racism in the South.

Grandma Helen stayed in Baltimore but had to struggle with racism and patriarchy. She didn't want to work for her father due to safety concerns, but he refused to let her quit. As she was underage, she worked with an ally to have herself emancipated. The fact that she managed to get this done as a Black teenager during those

times is mind-blowing and reminds me of the ancestors'
power of resilience.

The two met and got together in McKeesport.
Grandpa Herriott moved his whole family up north. They
were close and often spent time together. His sister,
Bessie Herriott, practiced hoodoo or a form of an African
Traditional Religion (ATR). My aunts said she "did weird
stuff" with tarot cards, money and witchcraft. I feel bad
they made her out to be crazy. I believe she's a huge part
of why I'm connected with hoodoo. I am honoring Aunt
Bessie because I reclaimed this practice!

My aunts told me stories of my ancestors laughing
and dancing. She mentioned that my grandmother and an
aunt had bad cramps. My grandmother was known in the
community for having strong medications to give girls for
their periods. My mother also had bad cramps.

Later in life, my mother and aunt were diagnosed
with endometriosis. To heal, my ancestors went to the

doctor, used castor oil for pain, prayed, and applied home remedies for colds: hot baths and saltwater. Before my grandmother, Grace Herriott Lloyd, passed, she was on a journey to eating healthier and using natural methods to heal. In a way I'm continuing her work in my journey.

All of this connected back to me. The issues with racism and white supremacy contribute to why my fight is so persistent. I inherit this from my ancestors. Additionally, the fact that they used Western medicine and holistic methods to heal, along with dealing with endometriosis, resonates with me. This realization led me to womb healing. I was healing myself, my ancestors, and my lineage.

As I healed, I healed my ancestors' old wounds. These practices showed my daughter how to heal herself and she can show her daughters and peers. I have gratitude for the ancestors for this download. However, the practices are in vain if I don't do them consistently.

*"Caring for myself is not self-indulgence,*

*it is self-preservation, and that is an act*

*of political warfare."*

~Audre Lourde, *A Burst of Light*

# RADICAL SELF-CARE

A huge part of my healing can be connected to me embracing Hoodoo, practicing radical self-care, and developing a rest practice. To me, Hoodoo was the answer I was looking for. In earlier chapters, I talked about feeling disconnected or out of sorts after the hysterectomy. Finding Hoodoo filled that gap. I didn't want to let go of this, so I continued my journey into becoming a Hoodoo practitioner.

This continued with me leaning more into the teachings of my ancestors and elders, which is a huge part of Hoodoo. I began to read books, essays, and articles. For example, Ancestor Audre Lorde first explored the concept of radical self-care. Specifically, in her collection of essays, *A Burst of Light*, she was battling cancer and wrote, "Caring for myself is not self-indulgence, it is self-preservation, and that is an act of political warfare." I studied this statement for weeks. It was unlike any other definition of self-care that I have ever read.

It connects more when you think about her battling a disease like cancer. I related so much to this. Battling endo can at times feel like a constant battle with pain with no relief in sight. The pain causes you to go numb and not feel anything. Not because you don't want to, because this shit HURTS. So, yes, when I rest, say no, or put my peace first, I am saving my own life. I took this concept personally and started to implement it.

**Setting Boundaries**

I developed boundaries and stuck to them, especially with work and family. You see, I was always the strong and responsible one. I do what is asked of me, typically more, and I keep my word. Folks became accustomed to this and would often gaslight my skill set against me.

They'd say things like, "When you work with Fawn, you have to work," or "She's always going to do what she says," and try to make me feel guilty for this. It was wild! I'd often feel like I was drowning in other people's expectations.

Taking inspiration from ancestor Lorde, for the first time, I fought against this. I started to say no, work an actual eight-hour day, only work on one to two projects at a time, and stopped being the one to call and check on others. I didn't come around unless I was asked. I didn't force ANYTHING. I mentioned this earlier, but I noticed no one was calling when it wasn't connected to my labor. It was lonely at times, but peaceful.

I stopped hanging around the "rest, until we need you" folks and sought out meaningful connections that were aligned. I made good use of the "block" button on my phone and social media. I had no chill with this, lol. At one point, I blocked my Mother, brother, and other relatives (I eventually did unblock them lol). To me, I was trying to save my life. So, I had no time to go back down old paths. I took my healing seriously.

I also took the time to develop a rest practice. And re-negotiate how I do my movement work. I can't stress enough that this goes beyond trips and getting your nails done. For Black women, this is essential for our survival. I understand that some may feel that they don't need to rest. And that Black women are magic and DOPE. Also, they believe we don't have time to rest.

I understand this thought process because yes, Black women are DOPE. However, we're also stressed and overworked. For example, suicide among Black women increased from 1999 to 2020, especially among Black teens and young adults, according to new researchers at Columbia University Mailman School of Public Health.

Furthermore, stress is a silent killer and can affect your heart. This is key due to the statistics on Black women and heart disease. The American Heart Association completed a study that showed that the prevalence of strokes for Black women is two times higher than that of white women.

I don't mean to sound harsh, but there comes a point where we need to get real with ourselves. Posting self-love content on social media does not mean you truly embody it. I am speaking from experience, as I have had to take steps to unlearn these behaviors. For a truly transformative change, we must go deeper. Black people can also walk and chew gum at the same time. So, yes, we can rest and still organize, as well as get things done.

Rest is a right that we all have. Capitalism has taken it away from us, but it's our inherent right to REST. For Black people, our relationship with rest, like so many other things, goes back to our ancestors, who were truly never allowed to rest. They spent 100+ years fighting and surviving the racial tragedies of slavery, Jim Crow, and the civil rights movement. They were not allowed to freely laugh, cry, or rest. That's why I believe when we rest our ancestors smile.

This is also something that should be done daily. This can look like prayer, meditation, hiking, or pausing and breathing for five minutes; whatever works best for you. Developing a rest practice will be beneficial for our growth as a people. It also allows time to think clearly and work more collectively. I can attest that it has been instrumental in my journey.

**Embracing Hoodoo**

When developing my personal rest practice, I looked to my ancestors and hoodoo. I continued on with ancestral veneration and put together an altar wall.

An altar wall may look different depending on the tradition, etc. Regardless of how you do it, the purpose is to invite your ancestors into your environment. These can be from your family or whomever you feel close to, or both. They can be inside or outside. None of this is right or wrong. The most important thing is to let the spirit and ancestors guide you in this process. I started with the obituaries that I kept. I never knew why, but after funerals, I'd sometimes keep the obituaries.

This is a practice that I started after my maternal grandmother, Grace, passed. I also kept her robe and Bible. Once again, I had no idea why, it just helped me feel closer to her.

I used the table that I had already kept the obituaries on. I laid a white cloth over it and added pictures of my ancestors, both from my lineage and some movement ancestors. I added sage, plants, essential oil, old objects of my ancestors, such as their Bibles, watches, lighters, and wallets. I also left water on the altar wall and used it for the plants.

Adding the element of water onto the wall made me think of a few things. First, the area I live in (McKeesport, PA), Mon Valley, has some of the worst air and water quality in the country. The majority of this is due to the steel mill and environmental racism. The same mill that my ancestors left the South to work at and "escape" racism. It's wild how those things connect. This is also important because I want to highlight the intersections of me battling endo, with me battling racism.

**Developing A Rest Practice**

The first time I sat in front of my altar wall, I thought of this. I used filtered water because I didn't want to use "toxic" water., I then just sat in stillness with them and asking for guidance. I felt their presence through the quietness. I also closed my eyes and meditated, which helped me to feel centered. I left feeling more alignment with my body and spirit. From here, I began to incorporate more into my rest practice.

Specifically, I would wake up early to ground myself and seek clarity. I go to my altar wall for 30 minutes to meditate, water my plants, and spend time alone with the Most High and the ancestors. On my altar wall, I have pictures of my ancestors, oils, sage, castor oil, and incense. In addition, I practice breathwork alongside meditation, drink water, and do yoga exercises. This combination helps with endometriosis pain.

I also changed what I was feeding myself. I changed the music I listened to. I made a new playlist with affirmation healing music. I highly recommend that you listen Toni Jones' affirmation music; it was on repeat in my house and the car. It healed things in me I didn't even have the words for. I joined a study group to begin reading books from my ancestors and elders on Black liberation. I opted to watch television for more positive entertainment not rooted in Black trauma.

I utilize breathing and meditation throughout the

day. Whenever I experience pain or feel the need to pause, I focus on my breath and meditate. Breathing helps my brain to calm down and return. I will note that while I learned all of this through reading, seeking out the elders and spiritual mentors, none of it would be possible if I didn't rest and FOCUS ON FAWN.

When I paused from fighting white supremacy, it allowed me to focus on myself. And yes, I kept and continue doing movement work. However, it's no longer the only thing I do. This clarity does not come without REST! Due to the current times, it will be more important than ever to understand this practice. Black people, especially Black women, I want you to learn from my experience and take the time to be intentional about unlearning white supremacy.

Go deeper, cry, laugh, and just be! Practice your radical self-care and heal in the fight.

## Growing and Evolving While Listening To My Ancestors

The more time I took to sit in stillness, the more I grew into my rest practice. As I mentioned before, I was working with a spiritual mentor. I credit my ancestors for connecting us. This started with the Windcall rest retreat, which I mentioned earlier.

I applied for twice and was turned down the first time. The second time, I was waitlisted, but someone dropped out. So, I was able to attend. At Windcall is where I became more open to the power of nature and the spirit. It's also where I met the people who introduced me to my mentor. Once again, a great example that all things are connected.

To start this process, my mentor gave me books to read: Stephanie Rose Bird's *The Healing Power of African American Spirituality* and Tayannah Lee McQuillar's *The Hoodoo Tarot: 78-Card Deck* and *Book for Rootworkers Cards*.

These books helped me to learn more and get a better understanding of the term "rest is resistance." I would spend hours reading and going "down a rabbit hole" for myself. Something new to me. As in the past, I would often dedicate this time to developing advocacy action plans to organize against racism. This was different, but I was proud of myself for continuing this practice. I also learned from some amazing teachers along the way.

I continued to work with my mentor on sound healing and meditation. I took a breathwork class from Mama Ayo Handy-Kendi and became a Certified Optimum Life Breathologist. Moreover, I did womb healing and Reiki from Mama Ifetayo White. In addition, I got certified in Embodied Social Justice. This led to me participating in Being Black, Healing Black with Rev. Angel Kyodo Williams. A powerful and healing experience with other Black activists, where we did some internal work to start the process of healing from racism.

I applied all of this to my life. I started writing again, which led me to having the courage to approach the New Pittsburgh Courier to do a monthly column and write this BOOK. I have found that writing this book has helped me with forgiving myself. I let go of people and things that no longer served me and welcomed rest and healing as a new way of doing my liberation work. Something that would become more needed as my endo journey continued.

*"I had become an expert of my body*

*and my pain."*

~Fawn Walker-Montgomery

# ENDO: THE GIFT THAT KEEPS ON GIVING

After my hysterectomy in 2022, I knew that it was not a cure for endo. However, I had no quality of life and made the tough decision to have it done. In late 2023, I started to feel some pain again. It wasn't as bad, but it was starting again.

My stomach doctor ran tests, which included a sonogram. The results showed that I had a small piece from an ovary that was left in. The medical term for this was ovarian remnant syndrome, or left-over remnant from the surgery. I had never heard of this and at first thought "oh great, another disease."

The doctor, who was one of the best endo surgeons, explained that this was at times common in people with stage 4 endo. This was due to the amount of legions they had to remove. The doctor also stated that it would decrease in size and go away on its own. While I appreciated his expertise, I went to my community and ancestors for guidance.

Specifically, I joined support groups on social media for people with endo and started my blog. The people who responded gave their opinions on their experience dealing with this. They all mentioned that it did go away, but some stated that it went away, came back, and grew. I was frustrated but thankful for their feedback. I then went back to my practice and went to my altar wall.

I heard a few messages. They were all rooted in me reconnecting with the power to heal myself. For me this looked like going back to my wall daily and not just every two days. Meditating more and just sitting in stillness. This led me to move into working with Mama Ayo on breathwork. I also insisted on getting follow-up sonograms, which showed that it did shrink. While dealing with this, I was also managing the onset of medical menopause, extremely intrusive tests, and the return of symptoms.

**The Gift That Keeps On Giving**

I was seeing endo as the gift that kept on giving. I say this because at that time it felt like it was always something. One thing after another, i.e., menopause and testing, etc.

For me, the menopause started with an aggressive change in body temperature. I would go from having a hot flash to being cold in minutes. The hot flashes were bad initially and would cause dizziness, nausea, and shortness of breath. I also had brain fog and would forget things in mid-sentence. This happened in the middle of some panels I sat on. The ancestors guided me to a local menopause clinic. They explained that it was due to menopause. This was comforting because I first thought, 'I'm getting old," lol. While the clinic made me feel seen, I once again disagreed with their advice.

The medical team there recommended that I take a pill, ORILISSA, to manage this. I, of course, did my research. The people in my support group shared unsettling stories of their experiences dealing with this that included losing cartilage, etc. I do recognize that this may be different for others. However, I had grown tired of using Western medicine and the long-term effects this had on my body.

Therefore, I leaned more into my ancestors, breathwork, CBD and meditation. I used castor oil to continue to draw out or shrink any remnants from the surgery, breathing to manage the pain, and stillness to hear answers. This helped me get through this and a brief occurrence with hives.

The doctors called them chronic hives and told me they would likely not go away. I went to my altar wall, used sound healing and a cream that came to me from my spiritual mentor, and oatmeal baths. After three months, the hives were gone. The doctors were in shock because they said they were chronic. During one of my doctor's visits, the PCP credited me for taking charge of my health and managing everything. She said, "Congratulations, Mrs. Montgomery, you survived." This was assuring and something I would need to remember moving forward.

I say that because while this was going on, I was still managing recurring symptoms. I had become an expert of my body and my pain. Therefore, I knew something was off. I pushed and asked questions to see if there was any testing that would show endo, without doing another laparoscopy (surgery).

There was, in fact, a test. An MRI that would show endo as long as a trained specialist viewed the results. I would later find out why this test was never brought up to me. This MRI was the most invasive and violating test I have ever experienced. It involved wrapping me in a protective case and placing things in both my vagina and rectum. They then put me in the MRI for 30-45 minutes. While in there I had to breath yes, breathwork, another download from the ancestors while they took pictures. Oh, and they also inject you with contrast. I have had four of these in the last two years. Afterwards, I would spend hours in the bathtub, sitting in the stillness. The MRIs showed that I did have a small patch of endometriosis in my lower right pelvic side. So, here I was fighting another battle with endometritis AGAIN!

*"I do recognize that there is no cure for endo. On the other hand, there are things you can do to stop it from spreading and taking over your life."*

~Fawn Walker-Montgomery

*"In the beginning, it was rough, and I had to ask the Most High to change my taste buds."*

~Fawn Walker Montgomery

# NOT FIGHTING MY PIVOT

The difference this time is that "I was no longer fighting my pivot." This is something that my best friend, Natalie, said to me as I was going through this. What she meant was  that I had been on rest journeys before, but I never stayed on them. I would start learning something but always get sucked back into fighting. After processing, I came to understand why she said this. I remembered the good things that happened with this journey and growth.

So, this time around, I was armed with my ancestors, breathwork, stillness, meditation, and the spirit. My doctors were recommending another surgery, this time in the rectum, to remove endometriosis they thought was there, as well as the endo in my pelvis.

When I say "remove," I mean take out the lesions

through excision surgery. I had done this a few times. Overall, I have had over ten inpatient and outpatient procedures due to endo. With this surgery, there was no way to know for sure that there was endo in my rectum; they could only judge the symptoms. This is because there is no test to show endo in the rectum. The only test is the MRI that showed the endo on my right pelvic area.

The thought of doing another procedure did not sit right with me. I went to my altar wall and heard that I needed to embrace eating.

**Food as Medicine**

Eating to some is a straightforward process. Everyone gets hungry, right, and we need food to survive. Well, for me and I'm sure others with endo, this is not an effortless process. When my endo got to its worst in 2021, I stopped eating a lot. This was because when I ate, it hurt. This caused me to lose weight. I would get compliments, and folks would ask what I have been doing to look this good. I'd think, well, I almost died from this horrible condition, so ya, here's that.

Of course, I didn't say that, but it was true. Even after the hysterectomy, this still occurred. Therefore, I had a weird relationship with food. So, when the ancestor told me to eat, I was confused at first. After sitting in stillness, I came to see that they were talking about what I was eating.

Meaning that I needed to re-evaluate what I was putting into my body. This messaging was in alignment with Hoodoo and African spirituality. In this tradition, detoxes combined with baths, heat, plants, and salt are practices passed down from our ancestors. Once again, I started to see the downloads.

Specifically, I had been using baths and heat this entire time. I would spend hours in the tub, sometimes doing Zoom calls. This is because the bath was one of the only times I wasn't in pain. Heat was another tool I had been using since the beginning. Often using heating pads or Salonpas, heated topical pads that get hot when applied to the skin. I had tried to change my eating and do detoxes a few times. However, as I said before, I had new tools this time.

I sought advice from a long-time healer, Queen Afua. I had two consultations with her. She utilized elemental readings to tell me things that I never told her. This was not the first time this had happened. My spiritual mentor would often say things I didn't tell her. This was due to their connection with the spirit and ancestors.

She communicated that I needed to do the full transformation into this lifestyle. Furthermore, I got the hysterectomy but didn't change anything about what I was eating. Also, I needed to be in a consistent community. To continue this, she had me start on her detox and on the path to becoming a coach. I did communicate that I wanted to do this for myself.

However, she understood that this would be something I would share with others.

The detox involved eating only fruits, vegetables, and juicing for 21 days. Also, turning your house into a wellness home. We went over what foods to eat for pain and other conditions. Being in a group of other Black women helped me to stay consistent.

For the first time, I was eating salads, fruits, and juicing consistently. In the beginning, it was rough, and I had to ask the Most High to change my taste buds. After two weeks, I noticed my hot flashes decreased, the pain was better, and my brain fog was less and less. I am in no way saying that this cured everything, or that it is some type of miracle. I do recognize that there is no cure for endo. On the other hand, there are things you can do to stop it from spreading and taking over your life.

For me, changing the way I ate helped with my condition. My endometriosis affected my stomach, and when inflammation occurred, it intensified the pain. Certain foods can cause inflammation. However, I want to emphasize that this may not be true for everyone. The most important thing is to find what works best for YOU.

I may have to get another procedure down the road, but I am blessed to have received these downloads and truly lean into healing myself. And not just myself, but my family and community.

# HEALING AT MY KITCHEN TABLE:

# NURTURING MY COMMUNITY

Throughout this book, you've heard me mention a few names that are part of my kitchen table, i.e., my mother, husband, daughter, and best friend. There are many others along the way who have impacted my life, from my sorority sisters of Delta Sigma Theta Sorority, Incorporated, Gamma Lambda Chapter, to childhood friends. In addition, those I met in college who became like family. Also, my siblings, aunts, cousins, and uncles. During the time I was battling endo, my mother's sister, my aunt, Dr. Valerie Harper, battled and overcame cancer. Watching her go through this and survive was a true inspiration for me.

Oddly, her daughter Nikki, who also has endo, was battling that and other diseases. Her comfort and being a listening ear through this were priceless. Also, my movement family: I have the pleasure of working with some badass organizers through my relationships at TAAG, Movement 4 Black Lives, and my socialist group. As I grew more in my healing journey, I noticed that this also helped my relationships and the healing of those around me.

Furthermore, this led to an improved relationship with my father. I was able to let go of my anger and forgive him for not raising us, etc. Once I did the emotional work to process these feelings, I could move past them and develop a relationship with him. This transformation led me to share these gifts and insights with the community.

As a longtime organizer, I first had to recognize that I had been healing my community. For years, I taught and showed people how to advocate for justice and wellness. I advocated for families as a social worker, and with my team at TAAG, we have helped countless families get justice from a system that was never designed for them. Now, I was just pivoting to show them a different way of healing.

I first observed this with my daughter, husband, best friend, and mother. I noticed that my daughter was resting more and taking naps. I would overhear her telling friends, "I need rest, so I am going to nap first." She says no when she needs to and even changed the way she advocates for herself in her relationships. Moreover, she started to change the way she ate.

This whole experience had a profound effect on her. I remember a time when we were in the emergency room. The doctor came in and said that my long COVID-19 had affected my lungs, and my endo was not curable. I knew this, but of course she was upset hearing it. At that moment, I told her that doctors don't have the final word, and with the help of the Most High and ancestors, I will heal and continue to progress. I'm blessed that she had a chance to see this happen. Moreover, even though she does not have endo, at times she gets bad cramps and uses some of these new methods to heal herself.

My husband fully embraced the softer side that came through when I accepted my higher self. I learned that being soft with myself would, in turn, allow me to give myself and others grace. This improved our relationship and helped with communication rooted in healing. Something similar occurred with my mother.

I noticed that she also let go of some people who no longer served her and formed new relationships. She was also open to doing breathwork and sound healing. My mother was one of the first people in my first wellness detox class. Additionally, she was a huge reason why I decided to heal publicly.

I remember a conversation we had after the endo came back. I was upset, and she asked, "Well, what have you been doing to survive? Keep doing that and share it with others." I took that as guidance, just as I did when I was little and she asked me how I would fight the racism in school. This time, though, I took it as an order to focus on myself. With this, I added wellness and healing into our work at TAAG.

We started doing wellness sessions with sound healing and yoga. I became a certified breath worker and detox holistic coach. I have gratitude that I can share this with my family and community. As I grow, how I do this work will continue to expand. A huge part of this will be sharing the knowledge I have gained about how to fight endometriosis.

*"Advocacy and organizing are our*

*superpowers. It SAVED my life.*

*If I didn't speak up, I wouldn't be here."*

~Fawn Walker-Montgomery

# ADVOCACY AND RESOURCES

A theme I'm sure you noticed in this book is the power of advocacy. I have alluded to this a few times. Advocacy and organizing are our superpowers. It SAVED my life. If I didn't speak up, I wouldn't be here. In this regard, many people have endo but don't know it.

This is especially true for Black women, due to medical gaslighting and racism, which are themes in the book. Contemporary OBGYN's study showed that Black women are only about half as likely to be diagnosed with endometriosis compared to white women. Furthermore, that "race may influence one's ability to access healthcare and obtain appropriate management for endometriosis." Something that I know all too well. Seeing stats like these helps me and other Black women with endo feel seen. Another good resource for this is the organization Endo Black, Incorporated.

Endo Black, Inc. is a Black-women-led nonprofit

advocating for and educating Black women living with and impacted by endometriosis. They were founded in 2015, 10 years after my diagnosis. I was able to find them when my endo developed into stage 4. They have valuable resources on their website, programming, an annual conference, and maintain social media support groups.

I joined all of them and have participated in one of their panels speaking about my hysterectomy. It's hard to put into words how transformative it is to heal alongside other Black women. This is because Black women aren't often allowed to rest and talk about things outside of our families and fighting for others. It amazes me when I tell my endo story, there is always another Black woman who has endo or endured a hysterectomy. Participating in advocacy groups were instrumental in my healing journey.

# NEW TOOLS AND TIPS

Throughout this book I talk about how my tools evolved from mainly using western medicine to Hoodoo, African spirituality and listening to my ancestors. I learned that no medical research or journal speaks louder or has more knowledge than the ancestors or my intuition. It's important to note that all of the tools, tips, and methods I mentioned only help to 'manage' my endometriosis; there is no cure for this chronic pain condition. However, finding a management method that works for you is crucial. The strategies I've shared are just a few that worked for me!

In previous chapters I mentioned how the ancestors used baths, breathing (breathwork) and castor oil to heal. I was using these methods before I knew it was a part of my connection to Hoodoo. The ancestors would do herbal and spiritual baths to heal. For me the baths were helpful to relax my spirit, mind and body.

I use warm water, with Epsom or Himalayan salt. While in the bath I would listen to meditation music, do breathwork, sit in stillness and say affirmations. Note that if you have high blood pressure use apple cider vinegar in the bath and not salt. In addition, I also do herbal baths with herbs and peppermint oil that helped with stomach discomfort (endo belly).

Other key tools and tips include having a personal journal that outlines your specific conditions, past treatments you have tried, and healers' or doctors' names. Take that to every appointment with a healer or doctor so you can document any improvements or concerns. Utilize medical communication tools the insurance companies typically provide, to communicate with doctors. This will help you to keep them accountable and make them do "their damn jobs."

It may sound like a lot to do, but so is dying, especially when it could have been prevented. The same way it's our duty to fight for our freedom and WIN, is the same way we have to fight for ourselves and WIN.

Seeking holistic and natural methods of healing were key as well. I mentioned a majority of these throughout the book. Other methods include obtaining a functional assessment from a holistic doctor. This is how I found out I had leaky gut. In addition, do not just depend on your gynecologist or endo specialist.

Make all of your doctors communicate and know about your condition. Also, ask your endo specialist for referrals to other endo-friendly doctors. This was helpful in my finding out that the endo caused me to get a slow-moving colon. For years, I thought it was me. I would have to jump around to produce a bowel movement. The detox and change in diet also helped with this.

Also, do your research in medical journals, support groups, and medical webinars. The support groups on Facebook and webinars were helpful to learn about new endo treatments. I often go there to ask before I try any new medicine etc. Countries like Australia do a lot of research on endo. And of course, eating fruits, veggies, and using CBD. This should be used as a treatment, and I will scream this from the rooftops. Lastly, if you are someone close to you, is dealing with endo, support them. If they are the 'strong friend,' listen to them the first time they share something. As someone who has been the strong friend, I understand how frustrating it is to have to repeat my story to those who are supposed to care. I remember having to recount my experiences again, only to hear people say, "Oh, I don't remember you mentioning that" or "Well, I knew you would get through it; you're strong." If you say things like, "You only have a few days to cry" or that it's time to "suck it up," you are minimizing their suffering. Let them rest and JUST BE. Educate yourself. Read and watch documentaries such as *Below The Belt*.

Outside of the other books I mentioned, it's also good to read Queen Afua's *Heal Thyself: For Health and Longevity and Circles of Wellness*. Like I have previously mentioned, take all of this information, but do what's best for YOU.

# CONCLUSION

## My Story Continues

This chapter is still being written. While I don't know what the future will look like for me, there are a few things that I do KNOW:

- I know it will be filled with Black joy, REST, and resisting, but not at the expense of my health. I can rest and resist!

- I know I'll continue my journey with endo while I grow, learn, and use this new way of fighting. Specifically, utilizing hoodoo, radical self-care, African spirituality, the Most High, and my ancestors.

- I know I'm more than my labor and I'm enough even when I am not WORKING.

- I know my ancestors and the Most High will always be there for me, if I sit still long enough to hear them.

- I know I must be consistent with radical self-care and

my rest practice.

- I know I do this healing work for my children's children. They'll be healed and will know they have the power to heal themselves!

I am grateful for this process. It has taught me that I am enough even when I am not being productive because I am resting.

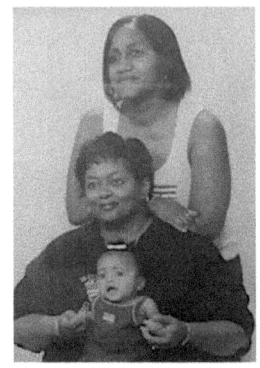

*Three Generations*
*Fawn with her mother,*
*Myrna and daughter, Grace*

Ase.

# APPENDIX

## *FAWN WITH FOLKS FROM HER*

## *KITCHEN TABLE + COMMUNITY*

## *WORK!*

Photos of my ancestors are courtesy of Sylvia

Samuels, my aunt.

| | | |
|---|---|---|
| *Helen Savage (Maternal Great Grandmother)* | *Thomas Briscoe (Helen Savage's second husband)* | *Charles Castelia Herriott (Maternal Great Grandfather)* |

*Fawn and George at TAAG's 10 year anniversary celebration.*

*Fawn and her family at a Herriott Briscoe Family Reunion*

*Fawn with Mae Herriott Hudson, Co-Founder of TAAG*

*Fawn's Passion/Community work with Take Action Advocacy Group formerly known as Take Action Mon Valley (pictured Soleil Meade, TAAG's Manager)*

*Fawn with her aunt, Dr. Valerie Harper and*
*Ancestor Uncle Daryl Harper*

# REFERENCES

- Afua, Queen. *Circles of Wellness*; Queen Afua, 2015

- Afua, Queen. *Heal Thyself: For Health and Longevity*; EWorld Inc., 2002

- Afua, Queen. Resources, Tips and Products https://www.queenafua.com

- American Heart Association. *Heart Disease and Stroke in Black Women, 13 February 2025,* https://www.goredforwomen.org/en/about-heart-disease-in-women/facts/heart-disease-in-black-women

- *Below The Belt.* Shannon Cohn, Director, March 2023. https://www.belowthebelt.film/

- Cleveland Clinic. *Laparoscopy, 1 March 2024,* https://my.clevelandclinic.org/health/procedures/4819-laparoscopy

- Columbia University Mailman School of Public Health. *Suicide Rates Among Black Women and Girls*

*Have Climbed for Two Decades*, 6 December 2023,

https://www.publichealth.columbia.edu/news/suicide-rates-among-black-women-girls-have-climbed-two-decades

- Denise, Candice: Self Care Coach

  https://stan.store/candicedenise

- Endo Black, Incorporated:

  https://www.endoblack.org

- Hersey, Tricia. *Rest Is Resistance*; Brown Spark, 2022.

- Jones, Toni. https://iamtonijones.com/

- JSTOR Daily. *The Combahee River Collective Statement: Annotated*, 24 March 2022,

  **https://daily.jstor.org/annotations-the-combahee-river-collective-statement**

- Kresser, Chris. *8 Dangers of Acetaminophen You Should Know*, 11 July 2019, https://chriskresser.com/the-dangers-of-acetaminophen

- Kronemyer, Bob. *How Race/Ethnicity Influences*

*Endometriosis,* 23 May 2019,

https://www.contemporaryobgyn.net/view/how-raceethnicity-influences-endometriosis

- Lee McQuillar, Tayannah. *Hoodoo Tarot: 78-Card Deck and Book for Root Workers*; Destiny Books, 2020.

- Lorde, Audre. *A Burst of Light: Essays.* Ithaca, N.Y. Firebrand Books, 1988.

-  Mayo Clinic. *Endometriosis Symptoms and Causes*, 30 August 2024, https://www.mayoclinic.org/diseases-conditions/endometriosis/symptoms-causes/syc-20354656

- Mayo Clinic. *Dilation and Curettage (D&C)*,
7 November 2023, https://www.mayoclinic.org/tests-procedures/dilation-and-curettage/about/pac-20384910

- Nunnelly, Shana: Sound Healing

  https://honeecomb.com/

- Rose Bird, Stephanie. *The Healing Power of African American Spirituality*; Hampton Roads, 2010.

- Walker-Montgomery, Fawn. *Unlearning White Supremacy, Part 2*, 12 April 2025, New Pittsburgh Courier https://newpittsburghcourier.com/2025/04/12/fawn-walker-montgomery-unlearning-white-supremacy-part-2/

- Walker-Montgomery, Fawn. *Is there an overemphasis on 'Black excellence' in Allegheny County? Part 1,* 7 May 2024, https://newpittsburghcourier.com/2024/05/07/fawn-walker-montgomery-is-there-an-overemphasis-on-black-excellence-in-allegheny-county-part-1

- Windcall Rest Residencies https://windcall.org

# GLOSSARY

Through the book I gave explanations on what these words mean to me. Here is a list of the words along with definitions and sources.

- *Abolition*-The act of officially ending or stopping something. https://www.merriam-webster.com

- *Advocacy*-The act or process of supporting a cause or proposal. https://www.merriam-webster.com

- *Ancestral Veneration*-A practice that is key to African spirituality. It takes many different forms and is tied to the traditional belief that ancestors' spirits remain in one's family and can intervene in human affairs. (Stephanie Rose Bird - Healing Power of African American Spirituality )

- *ASE* - (Pronounced Ah-Shay) originates from the Yoruba language of Nigeria and means affirmation or life force energy.

- https://www.thespiritualattorney.com/post/ase-what-it-is-and-why-its-important

- *Black Liberation:-*To help individuals in the Black community grow and prosper in mind, body and spirit by eliminating disproportional injustices that hinder Black advancement. Here you seek to build institutions that not only recognize Black humanity, but maximize the individual and collective liberties of Black people. (Take Action Advocacy Group, TAAG)

- *Gaslighting-*Psychological manipulation of a person usually over an extended period of time that causes the victim to question the validity of their own thoughts and perception of reality. https://www.merriam-webster.com

- *Hoodoo-* A culture, an inheritance, with a lineage in North America. The product of people who faced terrorism daily but, refused to give up. It's a body of botanical and esoteric knowledge, and a rebellion against mental and spiritual domination by Europeans. *(The Hoodoo Tarot: 78-Card Deck and Book for Rootworkers Cards, Tayannah Lee McQuillar.)*

- Internalized Ableism- The way that an individual absorbs and applies the beliefs and moral judgments of the dominant ableist culture, at a subconscious level. In other words, it's how we absorb and apply the beliefs our society has about disability to ourselves and others we see ourselves in. https://www.neurodiverging.com

- *Internalizing White Supremacy/ Internalized Racism-* The internalization of beliefs about racism and colonization that contribute to the acceptance of negative messaging or stereotypical misrepresentations that inform perceptions about worth and ability. Internalized racism is associated with psychological distress in racially diverse people. (National Library of Medicine)

- *Medical Gaslighting:*-An act that invalidates a patient's genuine clinical concern without proper medical evaluation, because of physician ignorance, implicit bias, or medical paternalism. (American Journal of Medicine)

- *Racial Gaslighting*- Researchers use the term "racial gaslighting" to describe a way of maintaining a pro-white/ anti-black balance in society, labelling those that challenge acts of racism as psychologically abnormal. (University of Cincinnati)

- *Racism*-Racism is a form of prejudice that generally includes negative emotional reactions to members of the group, acceptance of negative stereotypes, and racial discrimination against individuals. (American Physiological Association)

- Radical: Very extreme and different from the usual or traditional. (https://www.merriam-webster.com)

- *Radical Self Care*-Radical self-care is the prioritization of placing your needs before someone else's. (School Art Institute of Chicago )

- *White Supremacy*-An ideology that permeates many cultures through subtle biases built into society's institutions. (Psychology Today)

# ABOUT THE AUTHOR

As CEO of Fawn Walker-Montgomery Consulting and Take Action Advocacy Group (TAAG), an organization committed to advocating for Black liberation and social change, Fawn uses certifications in breathwork, embodied social justice, and detox wellness coaching to empower the community. Fawn has served as a senior clinician, therapist, and manager in social service agencies. She co-founded TAAG, and has 15+ years of experience in public service, social work, and community organizing.

A proud HBCU graduate of Johnson C. Smith University, and master's in criminal justice administration from Point Park University and is a member of Delta Sigma Theta Sorority, Incorporated.

Fawn lives in Pennsylvania with her husband, George, and they are the proud parents of Grace.

# STAY CONNECTED

Fawn Walker-Montgomery is available for speaking engagements, podcast interviews, and book club meetings. Feel free to connect with her on social media and leave a book review.

🌐 https://www.fawnwalker.net

✉ electvfawnwalker@gmail.com

📷 https://www.instagram.com/fawn_montgomery/

f https://www.facebook.com/vfawn.walkermontgomery

in https://www.linkedin.com/in/fawn-walker-montgomery-1458b7130/

substack fawnwalkermontgomery.substack.com

www.ingramcontent.com/pod-product-compliance
Lightning Source LLC
Chambersburg PA
CBHW051519120626
46551CB00012B/999